P9-CCW-571

Have Dog, Will Travel

Will Travel

A Poet's Journey

Stephen Kuusisto

Simon & Schuster

NEW YORK   LONDON   TORONTO
SYDNEY   NEW DELHI

South Huntington Public Library
145 Pidgeon Hill Road
Huntington Station, NY 11746

Simon & Schuster
1230 Avenue of the Americas
New York, NY 10020

Copyright © 2018 by Stephen Kuusisto

All rights reserved, including the right to reproduce this book or portions thereof in any form whatsoever. For information, address Simon & Schuster Subsidiary Rights Department, 1230 Avenue of the Americas, New York, NY 10020.

Several names and identifying characteristics have been changed, some individuals are composites, and certain events have been reordered.

First Simon & Schuster hardcover edition March 2018

SIMON & SCHUSTER and colophon are registered trademarks of Simon & Schuster, Inc.

For information about special discounts for bulk purchases, please contact Simon & Schuster Special Sales at 1-866-506-1949 or business@simonandschuster.com.

The Simon & Schuster Speakers Bureau can bring authors to your live event. For more information or to book an event, contact the Simon & Schuster Speakers Bureau at 1-866-248-3049 or visit our website at www.simonspeakers.com.

Interior design by Paul Dippolito

Manufactured in the United States of America

10 9 8 7 6 5 4 3 2 1

Library of Congress Cataloging-in-Publication Data is available.

ISBN 978-1-4516-8979-2
ISBN 978-1-4516-8981-5 (ebook)

In memory of Theodore "Ted" Zubrycki, pioneering guide-dog trainer and consummate friend of the blind. "Be good to yourselves, you deserve it."

Note to the Reader

In an effort to safeguard the privacy of several individuals, the author has changed some names and, in some cases, disguised identifying characteristics or created composite characters.

The ultimate definition of bravery is not being afraid of who you are.

—Chögyam Trungpa

Prologue

People ask: "What's it like?" "What's it like walking with a guide dog?" "How does a dog keep you from harm?" Or they say, "I don't think I could do that, I mean, what's it really like to trust a dog that way?"

Truthfully it's not like anything else. There's no true equivalent for the experience.

My wife is an equestrian. Years ago she was a guide-dog trainer. "On a horse," she says, "you're hypervigilant, aiming to avoid accidents by controlling your animal. Sometimes you and your horse will find a meditative rhythm. But you can't count on horses to look out for you."

A guide dog is not like a horse. She looks out for you. All the time.

What's it like? I can only help you imagine what a guide dog feels like.

Say you're in Italy in a swirl of motorbikes. It's Milan with thin sidewalks, confusing street crossings, and barbaric drivers. Montenapoleone Street is crowded with what seems like all the people in the world.

Let's say you're walking at night to the Duomo with Guiding Eyes "Corky" #3cc92. Corky does her thing and relishes her job. She pulls you along but the pull is steady and you feel like you're floating. Her mind and body transmit through a harness an omnidirectional confidence.

Why are you going to Milan's famous cathedral with a dog? One of your favorite books is Mark Twain's *The Innocents Abroad*, which contains passages so beautiful you sometimes recite them aloud. Of the Duomo Twain says it has "a delusion of frostwork that might vanish with a breath! . . . The central one of its five great doors is bordered with a bas-relief of birds and fruits and beasts and insects, which have been so ingeniously carved out of the marble that they seem like living creatures—and the figures are so numerous and the design so complex, that one might study it a week without exhausting its interest . . ."

Now it's just you and your dog. You're going there to touch the birds and fruits and beasts and insects carved from marble.

Not only are the streets teeming with people, there are skateboarders. Now your Labrador eases left. You hear a clatter of wheels. You think how Milan must be dangerous for skateboarding with its jagged paving bricks, broken sidewalks, and Vespas like runaway donkeys. Motorbikes plunge through crowds. Someone does a dance with death every twenty feet. The city is a fantastic, ghastly place. In the midst of this your dog is unflappable. Trained to estimate your combined width, she looks for advantages in the throng and pulls ahead because the way is clear or she slows suddenly because an elderly woman has drifted sideways into your path. Sometimes she stops on a dime, refusing to move. Which she does now.

There's a hole in the pavement. It's unmarked— there are no pylons or signs. A stranger says it's remarkable there aren't a dozen people at the bottom of the thing. Corky has saved you from breaking your neck. She backs away, turns, then pushes ahead.

It doesn't feel like driving a car. It's not like running. Sometimes I think it's a bit like swimming. A really long swim when you're buoyant and fast. There's no one else in the pool.

Yes, this is sort of what it's like, but there's something else—a keen affection between you and your dog, a mutual discernment. Together you've got the other's back.

Chapter One

I was late to the race, the opera, the prom—whatever you want to call it. I was terribly late. At thirty-eight, verging on middle age, having been blind since birth, I was not much of a disabled person. I was a second-rate traveler who didn't know how to go places independently. But late or not there I was, alertly hugging a yellow Labrador named Corky. We were brand spanking new to each other. We were an arranged marriage. We'd been together all of fifteen minutes.

"You're exactly what a dog should be," I said to her. "Your head's bigger than mine!" We were at a guide-dog school, a training center north of Manhattan. "Yes," I repeated, "you're what a dog should be."

It wasn't just Corky's size, though her largeness had merit—you want the dog who'll guide you through traffic to be sturdy. No, the "thing"—the ineffable "it," the "should"—was something like a welcome word. Maybe the word came from a distant room; the word had traveled a long way. So what if I'd been an unsuccessful disabled traveler? The dog before me, this Labrador, this superb creature didn't give a damn who I'd been or what I thought about myself. She was radiant.

*　*　*

Disability has numerous implications. One can live a long while recognizing only some of them. In the 1950s my parents couldn't imagine a future for me if I presented as blind. They forcefully encouraged me to do absolutely everything sighted children did, minus any acknowledgment of my difference. In the spring of 1961 my mother signed me up for the Durham, New Hampshire, Cub Scout troop and bought me a uniform and a flag. I marched in the Memorial Day parade, stepping in time to Boy Scout drummers. I held that flag straight before me and walked in a gorgeous gold mist, which was how my brand of blindness transmitted the world. I was legally blind. I saw colors and shapes.

"Who am I?" should always be answered by acknowledging physical life as much as say, knowing one's ancestry. But in 1961 a Boy Scout parade wasn't the place to learn about disability dignity and pedigree. The scouts' handbook didn't have a chapter about successful blind people.

I found it was best to not think about blunted sight—that's how it was. And I had help with my repression. None of the grown-ups in my life admitted disability. They'd come of age in the 1940s watching newsreels. In a famous (or infamous) short produced by the March of Dimes called *The Crippler* unsuspecting children were abducted by polio, who lurked as a menacing shadow—infantile paralysis was a molester at the playground's edge. My parents thought disabled kids were victims of a nearly unimaginable fate, a predatory darkness. Against this tragedy stood only human will.

There was a blind World War II veteran who lived a block from our house. My parents always referred to him as "the Blind Man" with tones of sadness and piety. The meaning was clear. I mustn't display vision loss, ever, for doing so would make me a victim of the Crippler. By today's standards this may seem quaint, but then again, even now I receive enough mail to know the story is still common. Many people across the globe still feel they must hide their disabilities.

* * *

We arrive at self-awareness according to thousands of influences. It took me years to see I wasn't a victim of a shadowy Crippler and that my parents' ideas about blindness were immaterial. In the twenty-first century self-determination for the disabled has grown from a nascent concept to a global movement. From Africa to Asia, Europe to the Middle East, disability activists are calling for their rights and living their lives in accord with the best principles of independence and empowerment—educating others, assisting their sisters and brothers, demanding opportunities for children, health care, freedom to travel . . . just to name the basics. The passage of the Americans with Disabilities Act in 1990 helped create international opportunities for dialogue between the disabled and served to incite a worldwide confrontation with outdated cultural assumptions.

Now at Guiding Eyes for the Blind, I had Corky's large paws on my shoulders.

Chapter Two

Essentially, on the day I met Guiding Eyes Corky #3cc92 the blind part of me was starving. Suddenly there was a dog—a "service dog," "guide dog," "seeing-eye dog," an epic dog, a professional dog, who was entirely my companion.

"Yes, it took me a long time to get here," I thought. But I could see Corky didn't care about my lengthy delay at all. She was interested in my left eyebrow, my fingers. She scented the history of my clothes. She was interested in me—the present-tense man, the one who was before her wearing sturdy L.L.Bean outdoor gear.

In order to meet Corky I'd had to suffer losses, wring my hands, and even sweat.

One minute I'd been a professor at a small liberal arts college in upstate New York. The next I was a job seeker whose teaching position had been erased. It's a routine story and ordinarily it shouldn't have been devastating but owing to blindness I couldn't simply switch gears and drive a cab or wait tables. Unemployment had pitched me in a dark wood with no discernible path.

The Dante analogy struck me as I drank coffee in a diner in Ithaca, New York. I was in a dark woods jam because I had absolutely no idea how to travel alone. I didn't know the first thing about visiting unfamiliar places without friends or relatives in tow. Pretending to see had been my one big trick and I'd been doing it with moderate success all my life. Sitting alone in the diner, killing time, worrying about how to live, I thought more deliberately than I often had about the art of pretending to see, how it had essentially always been a chicken game. In chicken, two automobile drivers race wildly toward each other. In blind chicken, the opposing driver is the world. While pretending to see, reality was my opposing driver. Would he quiver? Would "the real" step aside for my blind race? I'd always counted on it. Once, on a college study-abroad trip to the Greek islands, I rented a motorbike because my college pals were doing it. Some of them knew I couldn't see very well, or at least I imagined they knew, for while I paraded around without asking for help, I was halting and clumsy. But it was the late seventies:

no one had affirming language for disability, and hey, I was an unlikely guy and so were we all. We were on the island of Santorini—a steep crescent that rises from the sea. We rented Vespas in Fira from an old man who was listening to a football match on his radio and hardly noticed us. He didn't need to see our licenses, he only required cash and then we were off. I followed a student named Timothy who wore a bright red windbreaker. If I stayed close I could track him with my left eye. I saw a rectangle of red bobbing up and down. It was a flag in a bullfight. The sharp curves of Santorini wound like a ribbon under my wheels. I swayed and dipped but held the red flag in view. Unlike my classmates, I saw nothing of the panoramic ocean or cliffside ruins.

No one plays chicken because he feels good. When you play chicken with a disability you're trying to convince yourself you don't have a weak hand.

Someone once asked Lead Belly, the king of the twelve-string guitar, how he played the thing. "You gotta keep something moving all the time," he said. That's how you play sighted-man chicken when you can't see. You move. The faster the better.

Later I'd learn this game is prevalent among the

blind, since for obvious reasons many people are understandably reluctant to share how bad their vision really is. The sociologist Erving Goffman describes the dominant culture's view of disability as a "spoiled identity"—in a world where normalcy is a prerequisite to acceptance, nothing is worse than presenting an overt defect.

* * *

Hunched over coffee, frightened, I thought of how my aversion to blindness deserved a grand goodbye—and for a hundred reasons, some practical, some spiritual, I needed blindness to become a cherished personal effect.

I took out a Sharpie pen and wrote: *goodbye blind éclair, the one with the shame frosting; goodbye apologies—too many to name but let's be clear, I see how you've been stealing from my pockets . . . goodbye you circumspect opponents still living inside me—goodbye to you for now I'm stripping you of your sashes and medals . . .*

I heard my past in the diner, along with the scraping of forks on china and the tinny bell above the door.

* * *

The near past hadn't been much better than the long past. Losing my job had been ugly. I'd asked for a closed circuit TV device to magnify documents. The request was met with incredulity. A man in the treasurer's office said, "What if we buy the thing and rent it to you?" As if a reasonable accommodation was like a leased car. What if we charge you to work here?

"But yesterday is over," I thought. "The future, unknowable." I was having some blind Zen in a greasy spoon.

* * *

I'd worked all my life—had actually choreographed it—so I could travel to small and secure places without a white stick. I'd attended college at Hobart and William Smith in Geneva, New York, where my father was the president. I knew every inch of the campus. I learned in a private, ill-favored way how to walk mnemonically. It was eight steps down from the English Department to the sidewalk; seventeen steps to a funny break in that same sidewalk which somehow never got repaired; thirty steps between the post office entrance and my mailbox. I wandered by rote. At a school with only 1,600 students I could pretend to see. When I couldn't manage it, I'd say I had vision problems. Anything sounded better than blindness. I had "vision issues." I needed extra time to complete reading assignments. One of my eyes drifted. But still, seeing me move with intention from place to place, many friends and faculty had no idea how all encompassing my charade really was.

When I decided to attend graduate school at the University of Iowa's Writers' Workshop I flew to Iowa City three months early and walked the town like a crime-scene investigator. I walked in little grids. I moved haltingly up and down dozens of streets. When I thought no one was watching I drew a telescope from my pocket and read the street signs. I hiked in the stifling summer heat and worried about people marking me as deviant.

I was "Blind Pew," the untouchable, but I wouldn't let anyone know. By late August I knew enough of Iowa City to travel from my unfurnished apartment to the English-Philosophy building.

That was the summer I started keeping a journal. In July of 1978 I wrote:

If you love others you can be brave about your challenges. I am, of course, quite cowardly—I argue with friends, strain

relationships, talk too loudly, all because I hate my zig zag-
ging eyeballs . . .

I'm starting to think about the politics of bravery . . .
Would it kill me to mention in good company how much I
can't see?

It would still be some years before I could admit my
problems.

* * *

After grad school I taught poetry at Hobart and William Smith Colleges and extended my yearly appoint-
ment into an extended career. What a thing to be! A
blind fellow teaching literature in a small town.

Enter Dante. Overnight the woods. Though I'd often
been praised, I was an academic day laborer and "out"
with the stroke of a pen. Minus the capacity to go beyond rehearsed space, I was helpless. How could I move
to a strange city in search of a job?

A friend advised me to relocate to Ithaca, forty miles
south. It had a navigable downtown and I could learn
it. I traipsed Ithaca's sidewalks and followed strangers,
stopping when they stopped, moving when they moved.
I circled the city's center. I found my way to the famous

Moosewood vegetarian restaurant and sat beside a window and wrote poems in a notebook with a fat Magic Marker so I could see the results.

* * *

One morning I had a visit from a man who worked for the New York State Commission for the Blind. He was affable, even buoyant. He sat on my couch and bounced up and down. He said he wanted to help me find a new job. We discussed my résumé for twenty minutes and then without warning he said: "I don't think you'll ever find work." I sat across from him in a rocking chair and said nothing. I was quiet as a lump of moss. Then he added, just to break the silence, that he knew a company that made plastic lemons—the ones you find in the grocery with lemon juice inside. He said sometimes they hired blind people. I might be able to sort fake lemons. I saw myself in a dark shed wearing a suit made of starlight and juggling lemons.

When he left I sat for a long time. It seemed I had three problems. I was sad. I had to learn how to walk in a larger world. And I had to trust I could do this.

#200   04-23-2018 12:09PM
Item(s) checked out to p10437423.

TLE: Have dog, will travel : a poet's
CD: 30652005149853
E DATE: 05-14-18

*   *   *

There's an old Zen adage: if you want to get across the river, get across. I decided to start by going for a walk. It was a cold fall day and I moved through downtown Ithaca as I'd always done it, following people who looked like shadows. That's when I stepped into the path of a station wagon. A shadow had tricked me. The shadow had jumped ahead of the car and I'd followed.

I felt a brush of wind and found myself in the air, being pulled by a stranger. The stranger, my savior-stranger, was talking. I started to hear him. He said, "That was a Chevrolet. You were almost killed by a station wagon." I didn't know why this mattered but the car's brand seemed very important. It wasn't a Mercedes. It was a solid middle-class vehicle.

I sat on the sidewalk for a few minutes. I assured my savior I was okay. But sitting on the cement under a stop sign I knew there was no more room for deflection—if I wanted a big life, I needed a partner—a partner who cared entirely about my safety.

When I got home I dug up a pamphlet from Guiding Eyes for the Blind, a guide-dog school just forty minutes north of New York City. I'd acquired the brochure a few weeks earlier from a social worker. I called their number.

Little did I know I was about to enter guide-dog Corky's story.

Chapter Three

Aristotle described happiness as "human flourishing," which, he said, results from action and virtue. Both must be in accord with reason. Waiting for my class at guide-dog school I found myself thinking about virtue and reason. I wasn't genuinely old, but fearing how to live had made me prematurely tired. Reason and flourishing were, I thought, two long thin wings, like those of the osprey. I wanted uplift, possibility, and if flourishing had a preliminary step, I thought hope would be a good start.

I jotted notes about virtue and started drinking chrysanthemum tea at the suggestion of my friend Lu, a Chinese herbalist. Thick blossoms floated in the cup and sometimes petals went down my throat. The tea was meant to calm me. In fact I found I was starting to feel kind of cool—the temperature of my wiring was coming down. "That's because I've made a good decision," I told myself. Lu said it was also the tea. "Chrysanthemums cool the body and the mind," she said. "This," I thought, "must be one aspect of flourishing." I wrote: *It's likely Aristotle was cool all over.*

So waiting for my dog, a matter that would take around three to four months was actually satisfying. I'd made a true choice, a blossoming decision. Chrysanthemum tea was the drink of ironic accord.

Maybe it was the tea but I began seeing ironies everywhere. Early one morning I got a phone call from a field representative at Guiding Eyes who said his name was David See. "You work for a blindness organization and your name is See?" I said.

"Yeah," he said. "Ain't that nuts?"

He laughed. "I'm See," he said. "And now I want to see you."

Dave said he'd come to my apartment, interview me, and watch me walk around my neighborhood. I'd demonstrate what he called my "white cane" skills.

"Why do I have to display proficiency with a white cane?" I asked.

"We want our applicants to have good travel skills— to show they can make sound choices while walking," he said.

"But doesn't the guide dog do those things?" I asked.

"No," Dave said. "A guide dog assists you moving

from place to place but you have to know how to set the compass. Otherwise a guide dog is just a faster way to get lost!" I laughed, envisioning people with no idea where they might be going, all attached to fast-moving dogs.

Laughter aside, I wasn't about to tell Dave I had zero white-cane skills. We made a date to meet in four weeks and I hung up.

It was time to get serious. I called Mike Dillon, a well-regarded orientation and mobility teacher for the State of New York. Mike worked out of the Syracuse office, and was the nearest go-to person for Ithaca. His job was to instruct blind people how to travel safely.

Mike appeared on my doorstep the next week with a brand-new cane.

I was going to work hard to get to Guiding Eyes.

Mike handed me the cane and escorted me along snowy sidewalks. I told him I'd been faking vision all my life. "You know," I said, "faking sight is like being illiterate—you pretend to [have] competence but live by guesswork."

"Faking puts you at a terrible disadvantage," Mike said, adding I shouldn't trust my imagination.

We stood together in the winter cold and I found the curb with my stick. Mike had me repeat the production, sweeping the cane, locating the sidewalk's edge, finding the drop. I approached the curb several times. I made cane dots in the snow.

I was so self-conscious my skin felt tight. It was my mother. She was telling me to avoid being blind. She was saying it was shameful. Even though I was listening to Mike I was worrying about strangers: Did they see me from their front windows? Were people whispering about me? I imagined someone saying: "Look at that man with his white stick, how sad!"

Because I was absorbed with worry about strangers I could scarcely hear what Mike was saying about perpendicular traffic flow; four-way intersections; one-way and two-way streets. I made a conscious effort to forget the buzz in my head and concentrate. Eventually there'd be a dog. I was training for a dog. I strained to interpret traffic. I caught the myriad intricate noises of cars. The lesson—the goal—was to hear the directional flow of vehicles. In a world of twisted streets and inattentive drivers, the blind must be like high-wire artists, utterly steady. The snow was gusting. Mike watched my progress. I arrived at a corner where a group of laboring men waited for a bus. I found the curb with my cane. "Ese es su trabajo," one of them said. "That's his job."

Over several weeks Mike taught me to find the locus of my own freedom. I walked every part of Ithaca. I climbed steps at Cornell; rode the town's only escalator in a downtown mall; clamored on and off buses. I swept my cane from side to side, found a row of trash cans outside a pub. I stepped in a pot hole. I tripped on a pile of snow and walked into a street sign. I followed a path beside Cayuga Lake in a driving December wind. Freedom didn't really give a damn about the weather.

* * *

Andy Warhol said: "As soon as you stop wanting something you get it."

Walking with a cane, I didn't desire acceptance in my time-honored way. If waving a blind man's stick wasn't precisely liberating (as no manufactured object should hold such potent significance in my view), it was both useful and explanatory. In public I was just who I was. There was no pretending, no grasping for admission to normal-land. I pushed the cane from side to side and for the first time in my life I was in no immediate danger of being struck by a car. Moreover, I was powering a dynamo inside my head, a fanciful machine I pictured as throwing blue sparks—the electricity of forceful difference. My cane said I was unique but assertively so. I didn't care what others thought.

The arts of cane-walking and street-discernment were turning me, had turned me, loose from the impressions of others.

"What a goddamned thing to discover," I thought, "at thirty-eight I'm done with creeping."

* * *

When David See rang my doorbell three weeks later I was prepared. I was as ready for a test as I'd ever been.

We sat in my living room in the very chairs where the lemon factory man and I had discussed my joblessness. But Dave was as different from the lemon man as it was possible to be. He radiated confidence and he liked what he did.

Before we tackled the matter before us he asked what kind of music I liked. Though I'd cleaned my apartment in preparation for his visit there were lots of LPs and compact discs piled on my coffee table.

I wondered if it was a trick question. If I said "classical opera," would I be disqualified from getting a guide dog?

What about the Clash?

Dave was a muscular and outdoorsy kind of guy. He seemed like a Country Western type. I couldn't pretend to have any knowledge of country music.

"Eric Clapton," I said. "But not the Clapton of Cream—I prefer his days with Derek and the Dominoes.

"Ah!" he said. *"Got to get better in a little while!"*

"Exactly!" I said. "The sun's got to shine on my guitar someday!"

We laughed.

"So here's the thing," he suddenly said. "You've got a spotless apartment and very good taste in music, but are you sure you're ready to have a dog?"

"What do you mean by ready?" I asked.

"A guide dog is a huge responsibility," he said. "Even if you've had a pet dog before, this is a far more serious thing."

"Serious how?"

"Once you have a guide dog you'll be together almost every hour, every day. You'll have to observe strict rules and follow nonnegotiable guidelines," he said.

"You think you can handle that?" he asked.

"Yes," I said. No one had ever asked me to declare my maturity before.

"I can be that person," I said.

"Okay," he said. "I think you can too."

* * *

It was ten days before Christmas. Gusts of snow blew across the street as Dave and I set out. It was bitterly cold. Wind was masking traffic sounds. I worried I might cross an intersection against a red light or trip over a curb.

Dave's job was straightforward. He needed reassurance that I was a competent walker.

My task was tougher. I had to be skilled both inside and out—needed to have martial arts talents—to display balance, poise, and self-assurance. These weren't my strengths. But I was all in.

Then Dave hit me with something unexpected.

"Would you be willing to wear a blindfold?" he asked.

"Sure," I said, though the thought of navigating without my sliver of vision was scary—Mike and I hadn't trained for this and it felt like I was about to take a trigonometry test knowing nothing about the subject.

"I just want to see how you'll do under nighttime conditions when your residual vision isn't effective," Dave said.

"That sounds reasonable," I said.

Dave handed me an airplane sleep mask and I pulled it over my eyes.

"Is it tight?" he asked.

"It's nice and tight," I said.

"Okay," he said, "let's go!"

I set off walking east, wagging my stick, listening to cars and ambient noises—crows in a tree, a skateboarder, a truck grinding gears, two college girls laughing, a beeping traffic light.

With the blindfold I walked slower than usual.

"Can you go faster?" Dave asked.

"Yes," I said, and pushed my pace.

I lurched to a curb, found it with my foot.

I crossed the street successfully.

Somewhere on the next block I tumbled into a snowbank.

I leapt to my feet and forced myself to plunge ahead. I felt like a skater who'd lost his chance at a gold medal.

After ten minutes of sweaty work Dave told me to stop and remove the blindfold.

"You know you limp when you wear that thing," he said.

"I had no idea," I said.

"Yeah, you kind of drag your left leg," he said.

"You look like a peg-leg pirate," he said and laughed.

"It's okay, you were perfect. You have 'good cane,'" he said.

"You drifted sometimes because of the blindfold, which is why you tumbled into the snowbank, but really it was a good moment because when you got back on your feet you knew exactly how to reorient yourself and continue," he said.

* * *

So I'd passed my audition. I felt as if I'd undergone a "coming of age" ritual, the blindfold like a ceremonial mask. I'd danced with the ogre of happenstance and his brother the traffic spirit and I'd emerged intact.

Over coffee we discussed what would happen next.

"We're going to get started at the training center," Dave said. "Our job is to find a dog whose gait and temperament will be right for you."

"What does that involve?" I asked.

"Well, you're fairly athletic," Dave said. "So we'll want to give you a dog that moves along at a good pace."

"But wasn't I slow when wearing the blindfold?" I asked.

"Yes, but that was just an orientation test," he said. "Without the blindfold you move at a good clip."

"You'll also need a dog that can really go places," he said.

"Well don't they all go places?" I asked.

"Sure, but not all guide-dog teams have the same lifestyle," he said. "So for instance, some people never stray from their neighborhoods. Some people walk around the block and maybe go to the corner store. That's different from someone who wants to go to lots of distant places, who flies a lot, who has what I like to call *geographical ambition*."

He looked me square in the eye. "You have geographical ambition," he said.

I asked him if there was anything else I should do while waiting for my upcoming dog class. "You've got three months to kill," he said. "If I were you I'd hit the gym. You'll want to be in good shape."

Chapter Four

The evening before Dave's visit I talked with my mother who lived an hour west of Ithaca. There was a buzz on the phone line and she sounded drunk, though it was just dinnertime.

"I'm getting a guide dog," I said. My voice was high and happy—in effect I was a child saying "I'm getting a puppy!"

"Oh," she said, "I think that's a dreadful idea."

"Dreadful how?" I asked.

"People will know you're on the fritz," she said.

"On the fritz?" I repeated. "You mean like a household appliance?"

"Yes," she said, "you should never let people see you're defective. They'll think less of you." I announced I was excited and said she should think about that. Then I hung up.

I drank my chrysanthemum tea, chewed the blossoms, and understood my future dog shouldn't carry the burden of weak self-esteem. "No dog should have to do that," I thought.

*   *   *

My parents were essentially decent people who'd survived the Great Depression. Both were working-class kids and both went to college after the Second World War. My dad got his PhD in political science at Harvard in 1950. Having fought in the Pacific in the Army Air Corps he told my mother, "I need to learn how these damn things happen."

In turn my mother was accepted to law school in 1951, a true feat for any coed in those days, but instead she chose to raise a family. Later the decision haunted her. She belonged in a larger world than the one offered by postwar domesticity. She became a housewife in Durham, New Hampshire, a college town, and became a hostess for faculty parties.

No one knew how to confer about difficult or liminal subjects. Not talking became its own drama. As I grew up I formed an antinarrative. My parents' silence about my eyes sent me in two directions. One was physical and daring. The other was inward and bitter. When climbing trees or becoming the unchallenged king of hide-and-seek I secretly knew I was the most deficient child alive. The feeling, however wrong, didn't get better as I grew older.

"If I'm going to get a guide dog," I thought, "then I need to do more than just hit the gym." I needed to access my proper life—not academic life; not something from the Gospels. I would vanquish old embarrassments. As I set out on my dog journey I knew it was time.

* * *

When I was twelve, my mother, who'd already become a heavy drinker, met me one afternoon as I came home. I'd hoped to find safety after seven hours of bullying in school.

Instead I found my mother clutching a smoldering sofa cushion in her arms. "I don't know how I did it," she said. "Get out of my way!"

She ran across the yard holding the thing at arm's length and for some reason she didn't drop it. She just staggered from place to place until flames singed her hair. Finally she threw it into a neighbor's hedge, where it sent up smoke signals.

That was a gradient point on the arc of withdrawal.

My job was to endure by stamina whether in school or at home. So blindness became a tortoise-like affair. My blind soul stayed quiet in its shell.

My mother was generally drunk by midafternoon. Like most alcoholics she had several modes of intoxication. There was a giddy vaporous kind born from merriment. Then there was a drunkenness forced by what I came to call her misery gauge—I pictured a glass indicator on a submarine—pressure was building against the hull. She also engaged in vengeful drinking, the kind Nixon did as president, a mumbling paranoia.

If I was lucky, she'd be asleep when I came home, stretched on the living room sofa with the curtains drawn, her highball glass on the floor, and one shoe off. I'd race to my room, lock the door, and strip off my torn shirt—for daily bullying always meant the death of a shirt. I'd lie on the rug and listen to the shortwave radio. There was a station from Belgium that played only Duke Ellington. Something in his music felt right to me—the Duke was complex, buoyant, I didn't know what to call it, but I always luxuriated in it.

Because my father was an academic, and moderately less guarded than my mother who refused to talk about my eyes, he told a colleague just how little I could see. One night he came home with a large cardboard box containing a dozen sealed and labeled mason jars—his friend was a scientist of some kind and the jars held dark specimens floating in formaldehyde. The idea was that I could hold the jars close to my one good eye and see things.

Alone in a circle of lamplight, I held the first jar close to my face. A white human fetus floated in viscous brown liquid, trailing its umbilical cord. The jar was so near my left eye my eyelashes brushed the glass, and owing to my shaking hands the fetus turned gently, that gentleness of the drowned, until its face was straight opposite my cornea. It had gray veins across its temples and a determined frown. I thrust the jar back in the box. I wanted to go downstairs and tell my father to take it away but he was fighting with my mother and I shoved the whole collection into the back of my closet behind a heap of shoes.

After that I lay in bed knowing the fetus was in my closet, suspended in its soup with its little face all closed up.

* * *

I wanted to grow my hair long like the Beatles' guitarist George Harrison. In public I was a mark. Boys stole my glasses, pushed me into walls, shoved me on the stairs, all because I was the deviant. I could feel their contempt all the way down to my spleen. Long hair would save me.

My mother was painfully drunk when she called me for supper one evening. Before I knew it, she had me in an armlock and was dragging me across the kitchen.

"You look like a fairy," she said.

"What's a fairy?" I asked. I really had no idea.

"A faggot!" she said.

She was blowing whiskey vapor, clutching my hair, poking my skull with scissors. I pushed her. She fell backwards waving her shears and fell into the trash. Because she hated domesticity she'd long ago decided a thirty-gallon garbage can was perfect for the kitchen; you didn't have to empty it daily, and of course it stank and then she was in it.

I should say it's quite likely she'd have fallen into the trash without my help, as she was always unsteady on her feet, drunk or sober.

The can tipped over as she fell and the lid popped off and together she and the can had a rendezvous and there she was, covered with mire and ashes and waving the pruning scissors and howling. She'd bruised her elbow. I was the inciting factor. In the weeks that followed I was the one who ruined her elbow.

* * *

With three months to go before guide-dog school I decided to attend Al Anon meetings. I wanted to be new both inside and out. An offshoot of Alcoholics Anonymous, Al Anon is designed to help the families of drunks. A group of strangers, seven of us, sat around a scarred table in a community center in downtown Ithaca. There were coffee cups at hand and ashtrays.

A woman in her late seventies named Margaret, who'd once been an Atlantic fisherwoman and radiated competence, spoke up and recited lines from Ephesians:

"Let all bitterness, and wrath, and anger, and clamor, and evil speaking, be put away from you, with all malice . . ."

Margaret looked up from her Bible and said, "Now ain't that the truth!"

We laughed. Everyone at that table had once lived with or was still living with a drunk. Each had bargained meager coins of the psyche while living with a dramatic, angry, and addicted person and often more than one of them.

Margaret's former husband was also a fisherman and a boisterous drunk who once stole a trolley filled with passengers when the motorman stopped to take a leak.

"The cops chased that streetcar for blocks while Bert sang filthy songs and demonstrated uncommon driving skills. They finally cut off the electricity and cornered him. Some people said it was the best ride they'd ever had."

That was the thing. We all agreed. Drunks are vivid, manipulative, and dramatic. They can convince you of anything.

Until being convinced becomes your job.

So I told them about my blindness and how I'd lived according to my mother.

Margaret and I reckoned that Bert and my mother would get along famously. Both believed in swashbuckling with whiskey and believed mind over matter makes the world go around.

It was Margaret who said what should have been obvious: If I wasn't blind then my mother wouldn't have anything to feel guilty about. Moreover, if I wasn't blind, if I never actually went anywhere, then I could look after her.

"It's the old love-hate dance all drunks waltz to," she said. "Alcoholics love their own guilt," she added. "It gives them reasons to keep drinking."

Chapter Five

Four months had passed since Dave See's visit. It was early March and snow was falling as I arrived at Guiding Eyes for the Blind in suburban Westchester County, a forty-minute drive north of New York City.

Though my vision wasn't seriously reliable, I noticed the pleasant grounds with old trees, a white colonial house, and a neat brick dormitory. Nearby stood a veterinary hospital. Guiding Eyes looked like a small community college.

"You must be Steve," someone said as I stepped from the airport shuttle. "I'm Linda," she said.

"Welcome. I'm one of the trainers."

"Great," I said. "Is it okay if I admit I'm kind of nervous?"

"Well the dogs never bite," she said, laughing, "but you never know about the trainers."

"C'mon," she said, "I'll show you to your room."

As we walked Linda asked questions about my type of blindness. There are hundreds of blindnesses and no two people experience vision loss the same way. Linda was asking "How is it for you?"

"It's like I have Vaseline in my eyes," I said. "Up close, pressing my nose on a printed page, I can read large print—but only with one eye."

"You know there are so many variants of the low vision–no vision experience," Linda said. "I'm amazed by every blind person who navigates this planet."

It was such a simple thing to say and yet I was truly warmed. There we were, the two of us simply standing in a dormitory hallway and for the first time in my life someone had affirmed what it was like to be me. I'd been in the building sixty seconds.

I remembered John Prine's great folk song about aging—"Hello In There." A person who didn't know me was acknowledging my existence.

My room had a dog crate and a wall-mounted radio with oversized tactile buttons. There was a back door that opened onto a cement sidewalk where we'd be relieving our dogs when the time came. "The dogs have been trained to do their business on cement," Linda said.

Linda then left me to unpack. She said students and trainers would meet together in one hour. I thanked her and after she left I wrote a few lines in my journal:

March 1, 1994:

I have an hour to kill before the first group meeting.

This is a good time to think about trust . . .

Trust probably has something to do with luck—as in, making peace with it . . .

I've grown up not thinking of luck. Like most Americans I've imagined I'll get ahead by thinking my way forward.

I think this might be a place where people know a lot about trust.

* * *

Before arriving at guide-dog school I actually thought I'd be handed a dog who knew some commands and that would be it. It would be simple. Looking back, if I'd known how much my life was about to change I might have experienced some apprehension. I was going to be enlarged in several ways. All I knew for sure on day one was that I'd made a commitment.

At our first group meeting I saw we were old and young, American and Israeli, men and women, northern and southern. Some of us were kids straight out of high school. We were black and white, Latina. One of us was very tall. Four of us had already had a guide dog.

The rest were newbies. Everyone was chatting. The simmer of talk was pleasing.

We were Tina, Mike, Aaron, Joseph; we were Harriet, Doug, Constance, Sally; Jeff, Anna, Bill, and Steve. The trainers were Linda and Kylie and Hank and Brett. We were drawn together not just by blindness but also because training with a guide dog is about the future.

Linda called the meeting to order.

She said: "Let's talk about dogs. Let's talk about how tomorrow is going to unfold."

"Oh boy, dogs!" someone said. Everyone laughed.

Linda turned to trainer Kylie and said, "I don't know, do you think we have any dogs here?"

"I think I saw one," Kylie said.

"Probably a stray," Linda said.

"Okay, jokes aside," said Linda, "tomorrow, we'll ask each of you to take a walk with us. The trainers will pretend to be guide dogs. Our goal is to get a sense of your walking gait, your speed, and what kind of pull is comfortable for you."

She explained there were multiple dogs "in waiting"— dogs "all trained up" and ready to go.

There were twenty-four dogs for twelve students.

"Just as no two human beings are alike, no two dogs are the same," Linda said.

"Part of a trainer's job is match-making," she said, "knowing which dog will fit each and every one of you."

"In the morning we'll walk the grounds of the school. Trainers will move fast and pull the front end of a dog harness, and you're going to hold the handle and pretend you're walking a real guide dog."

I wasn't sure what I thought about walking around with a "pretend" guide dog. Somehow it seemed embarrassing, oddly performative, but my comfort wasn't as important as my safety, and ultimately getting the right dog. This much I knew.

* * *

At eight the next morning I stood beside a fountain with Kylie, who was ready to be my dog. I was going to walk a harnessed woman around a parking lot.

Once, in college, a friend persuaded me to help him walk about in a donkey suit. We were going to perform at a children's fair. My job was to hold up the back end. "It would be perfect," my friend said. I didn't have to see, just keep myself upright. Of course the problem was my friend couldn't see either. The eye slits kept shifting. We stumbled into a trash can. We walked over a beach blanket and broke a toy. I grasped my friend's arm. He staggered. I laughed so hard I fell out of the donkey and lay on the grass. "Look," someone said. "The donkey has given birth to an idiot!"

I thought, "Okay, I can be the back-end fool."

"When I'm a good dog you're going to tell me," said Kylie. "When I'm a bad dog you're going to give me a correction with this leash." She showed me the leash.

"How will I know when you're a bad dog?" I asked.

"I'll stop when we're supposed to be walking because I want to sniff the grass," she said. "Or I'll veer off the path."

"And what do I do with the leash?"

"You're going to give it a tug and you're going to say 'no, hup up!'"

"Hup up?"

"Yes, hup up."

"What does that mean?" I asked.

"It's an old guide-dog command, it tells your dog to refocus."

"Kind of like a reset button?"

"Exactly."

"Does it mean anything else?" I asked.

"Yes, it can mean it's time to go faster."

She went on to explain that when she stopped for curbs or steps I should praise her. For the purpose of the exercise her imaginary dog name was "Juno."

"All the guide-dog schools use the name Juno for this exercise," she said. "There's no real guide dog named Juno."

"Juno," I thought, "Roman goddess of war, fertility, and youth." It was one of those throwaway thoughts. Juno. Juno. Make me young.

"Are you ready?" she asked.

"Okay," I said, "let's go."

We walked and Kylie pulled with steady force—"a real guide dog," she said, "will pull. They're not like pets trained to heel. The pull allows your dog to have fluid movement as you're walking. She'll see an obstacle and guide you around it without breaking stride. You'll also learn during training that the pull creates a trust factor."

"Yes," I thought. "Trust. My weakest area."

"Good dog, Juno!" I said as Kylie stopped at a curb.

"Now you're going to tell her to go forward," Kylie said.

"Juno, forward," I said.

Off we went. We veered and zigged and zagged—I said "hup up" when Kylie turned toward a flower bed. We recommenced our little journey.

When our Juno walk was over Kylie said I had a good handling technique. I had no idea what this meant. She also said I was a speedy walker.

That night I wrote in my journal:

Can trust be taught? Is trust related to embarrassment? Maybe I should have risked more embarrassment in my life?
   Tomorrow is dog day.

* * *

By the second day I'd come to see Guiding Eyes as a sailing vessel. It was a contained and intense place. We were on the ocean together, trainers, students, and dogs. At 6 a.m. the intercom crackled. It was time to hit the deck. There'd be a morning class and then in the afternoon we'd be given our dogs. I stumbled around my room. I hit my head on the bathroom door. I rubbed my brow and thought, even with a poor start, this was a different day from all others—it was dog day. "Dog day,"

I thought, "is like getting married but it's an arranged wedding—the bride and groom don't know each other."

Our first class was about technique. Everyone received a stiff leather leash. We learned how to use brass clips and rings to make it long or short. "The short leash," said Linda "is for working dogs in harness. You'll learn more about this tomorrow—the short leash is kind of like a dog's throttle and brake. The long leash is for potty breaks or letting your dog sniff the grass." We practiced making our leashes long and short.

We learned the proper command to encourage a dog to relieve itself. "Get busy!" It felt silly to say it but we did.

"Guide dogs," said Linda "will 'get busy' on pavement or cement—they don't need grass."

"Now we need to talk about your dogs," Kylie said.

"Later on this afternoon each of you will be united with your dog. Remember, this will be as powerful and beautiful for her as it is for you. When we release her you're going to call. She'll be excited—she may come straight to you, or she might run in circles before she comes—she's been in a kennel for months, working each day with her trainer. Today will be something new for her as well.

47

"By the way," Kylie said, "I'm using her when speaking of the dogs, but half the dogs in this class are male. There is absolutely no quality distinction between the genders—both male and female guide dogs are equally good at their jobs."

Linda added: "All the dogs in the class are Labrador retrievers. Some are black Labs, some are yellow. There's no difference between them—in fact they occur in the same litter of puppies. Some of the dogs are big, some are smaller—again, there's no difference.

"Don't compare your dogs," said Linda.

"Your dog won't be better because it has a longer tail than your neighbor's dog. This is a group activity requiring encouragement."

"Well," I thought, "here's where a guide-dog school isn't like the navy—no admiral describes a flotilla as a matter of encouragement."

"The next three and a half weeks will be stressful, engaged, tiring, and even thrilling, but the goal behind everything we do is to see that you and your new dog become a superb team. Your dogs need encouragement. And so do you. And you should give it to each other," Linda said.

I thought of lines from Dickens's *Oliver Twist*: "For

the rest of his life, Oliver Twist remembers a single word of blessing spoken to him by another child because this word stood out so strikingly from the consistent discouragement around him."

"A single word of blessing," I thought. "A single word of blessing."

The trainers shifted gears. "Now we're going to tell you the name and color of your dog," said Kylie.

"The dogs were named at birth—and each litter of puppies receives a letter of the alphabet. Every dog in the litter has a name beginning with the designated letter," said Linda.

"Some of the names are a bit unusual," said Kylie. "We name a lot of dogs."

"In other words, don't get wigged out about your dog's name," said Linda. "Your dog likes her name."

The names of our soon-to-be dogs were read aloud.

The names were at once splendid and silly: "Tinsel"; "Abby"; "Norway"; "Tammy"; "Henry"; "Whisper"; "Captain"; "Johnny"—I was amazed by the silly nature of the names—who'd have thought a hero dog would be named "Whisper"?

"Steve, your dog is a yellow Lab named Corky," said Kylie.

"Corky," I thought. Wasn't there a killer whale named Corky? It seemed both carefree and tough. Perhaps that's how we'd be together?

Our dogs were going to have baths, Linda said. Then we'd be united with them one by one.

* * *

I waited in my room and imagined a map—a "might be" map of life to come. What if the future would be okay? What if it would be truly lovely? What if having a guide dog "worked" for me? I saw these were the proper things to think about. And then my name was called via loudspeaker and it was my turn to meet Corky. I grabbed the leash and walked to the lounge.

* * *

Corky burst in like a clown. I sat in a tall armchair and Kylie told me to call and damned if she didn't run full steam into my arms. She placed her large front paws on my shoulders and washed my face, and then, as if she fully understood her job would require comedy, she nibbled my nose.

She was brilliant and silly. I couldn't believe my luck. Back in our room she bounced, cocked her head, backed up, ran in circles, and came back. All the while I kept talking. "Oh let's go anyplace we choose," I said, feeling I was on the verge of tears.

As our first hours unfolded we began the lifelong art of learning to read each other.

She was happy but she had something else, a quality of absorption. She looked me over like a tailor. She took me in. She wasn't searching for a ball to be thrown. Was it my imagination or did she actually have the most comprehending face I'd ever met?

There are times when you can't describe your feelings. You say, "So this is the new life."

I thought: "So this is the new man with the big dog—the big yellow dog, who cares not a whit about the old man's history and already believes in his goodness."

Chapter Six

At a traditional university students listen to professors and take notes, but at a dog college you and your canine sidekick are handed the tools to live your lives.

Our first lecture was about praise. Sitting with Corky and the other students I realized that despite my thirty-nine years no one had ever taught me a thing about praise. Here we were, a bunch of young and old blind strangers, dogs, and dog trainers, together, in a room talking about admiration.

Linda sat before us with a leash in her hands.

"Our dogs are gentle," she said.

This was not hard to believe.

"Our dogs are gentle because their breeding has changed. If you're an old-time guide-dog user you need to know that things are different with today's dogs."

There were murmurs from some of the long-timers. A few of the students had been guide-dog travelers since the early sixties and they were used to a different kind of guide—"hard dogs," as they liked to call them.

The old-time students were being told today's guide dogs were softer and required more subtle handling.

"Our new dogs require praise—lots of praise," said Linda. "It's all in the voice. Nowadays a guide dog loves it when you say 'Good dog' with a tone of true joy. Try it!" And we all said "Good dog," just as Linda had shown us.

Corky raised her face to look at me, her big yellow snout pointing straight up. And every dog in the room did the same. Something palpable went around our circle—the star of praise that only dogs can see was released by our voices. "Good dog!" We said it again and again. Our overdramatized tones were like stylized laughter in an opera. All tails were wagging.

"We say 'Good dog' because Guiding Eyes dogs really want to work," said Linda. "They have been through many months of training. These dogs enjoy their jobs. But just like you, they require praise. From this moment on you will be saying 'Good dog' as much as a hundred times a day."

Who affirms good things even a dozen times a day? Who makes "talking goodness" a habit of her or his minutes? I sat with my Corky's head on my shoe and thought about the "talking blues"—as a literary guy

I'd studied vocal sorrow—but never had I considered a running, day-long practice of spoken good. "Good dog" would become my hourly practice and over time (though I didn't yet know it), dog-praise would change many of my habits of thought.

"You're going to say 'Good dog' when you come to a flight of stairs and she stops; you'll say it when she comes to a curb and waits; you'll say it again on the far side of the street when she shows you the up curb. You'll say it when she sits obediently in a bank or post office; when she ignores strangers; when she walks past a fenced yard full of barking dogs."

We practiced it then, praise, undiluted, with rising notes.

*　*　*

"Praise of various levels and types can be perceived differently by each individual dog," Linda said.

"Inflection of praise is so important. We call this 'directive praise.'"

Some of my classmates were taking notes with talking laptop computers. I could hear sparks of machine-generated language. I heard someone's dog sigh. I also heard sleet striking the far windows. It was a cold day in March and we were sitting close together in a warm place hearing from a great dog master about the qualities of praise and the lives of dogs. I was happy. I realized I didn't need to take notes.

Linda continued to explain:

"Directive praise is not light and bubbly. It's motivating and straightforward, but at the same time neutral. That means the praise holds no emotion in any direction. Your dog thinks: my handler is comfortable, and relaxed, so am I. If the inflection of the praise drops or changes suddenly, then the dog may perceive this as something wrong, or that something uncomfortable is coming up. If the praise becomes excitable, then the dog may leave its comfort zone and become stimulated over the handler."

I remembered a college professor who said in a class on Buddhism: "Many people think excitement is happiness, but when you're excited you're not peaceful, and true happiness comes from peace." Dog-praise would have to be peaceful.

I saw that becoming a dog man would require becoming an amateur Buddhist.

"Every person in this room is unique," Linda said then. "And every dog is unique. Praise is what brings each team success. Praise is the secret ingredient. You're all going to bond through praise.

"From your dog's perspective we can look at praise in three ways: it motivates and directs to a goal, it validates a correct choice, and it reaffirms what the dog already knows."

"Amen to that," I thought.

* * *

I wanted to be equal to Corky's sweet alacrity. My goal was to be warm and steady for her. By day two at dog college my thoughts were turning empathetic. "What does it mean," I thought, "to be purposeful and loving?" In the coming days I'd learn what Corky knew—learn that praise and motion, praise and accomplishment are synonymous and find that as I praised her I was praising us.

"Good dog!" I said. We walked the hallways of the dormitory. "Step one was just saying it—good dog, good man—good for simply doing what you do." Each step is good. Every footfall. "Walk as if you are kissing the Earth with your feet," said Thich Nhat Hanh, a Zen master whose writings I'd always loved. "Now walk as if you are kissing the Earth with six feet," I thought, "and say, 'Good dog!'"

We were moving slowly and loosely. We were ambling, getting to know each other. "Your work is to discover your work and then with all your heart to give yourself to it," said Buddha. It was clear that my job would be to discover life with a dog and this would be walking, open-minded work.

* * *

By the third day I was already large with affection. "Boy, you two look great together," said Linda as we entered the dining room. "Corky's really in love! Look at her face!" I felt the praise and it warmed my insides like brandy. "Make sure," said Linda, "that you don't choke up on her training collar, just be loose."

"Dare to be loose," I told myself.

On the way to breakfast I saw each moment was about practice. Walking to meals we made our dogs sit at the bottom of the dining room steps. Then, one by one, we heeled them up the stairs as Linda observed our form. "Give your dog a little more leash," she said, because Sally was choking her wiggly Lab, "just tell her to heel and say 'Good dog'—she knows what to do." Each instant taught us lessons about how to live with a dog always at our sides. As I buttered my toast I thought: "I will be with a dog every minute. Life will always be a man-dog arrangement from this moment onward." I knew something beautiful and fortunate was happening to me and I reached down and touched Corky's ears.

* * *

Yes, the "very here and now" was fascinating. There was an art to the smallest things. Boarding a van for a trip into the field we learned to make dogs sit as we climbed the short steps, then to call. "There's a protocol for getting on and off public transportation," said Linda. "You don't want your dog bounding ahead and tripping you up." The coordinates of dog training and daily activities were seamlessly connected, beckoning a stronger awareness of self for every one of the students. We learned how to put our dogs under seats; how to gently put on and take off their harnesses; how to give them small treats as rewards; how to "love them up"; how to be firm; in effect, how to become superb life-teams. Practicing putting Corky's harness on and taking it off I thought: "Stability, freedom, harness, self," and resolved to write it in my notebook.

* * *

Things were moving fast. We were all traveling to the city of White Plains together in a twelve-passenger van, people and dogs. We were going to work the dogs in traffic for the first time. We were all in good humor. Linda and Kylie sparred with Sally and Tina about the merits of "Karma Chameleon" by Culture Club, which was playing on the radio. Kylie and Tina were fans, Linda and Sally thought he was a sham. I knew nothing about Boy George. I thought the song was catchy, but I kept silent. I loved the mock seriousness of the debate. Their banter reminded me just how much one can love human beings. People can be exceptionally beautiful when they're silly and trusting and working as a team. "Maybe baseball players experience this?" I thought. I'd never actually done anything that involved teamwork before.

Corky was tucked safely under my seat. I reached down and ran my hands over her face. Her nose was wet, like a strawberry, but with dimples and adjacent whiskers. Her snout had peachy fur but was also tough with cartilage and tiny hidden turbinate bones. My fingertips reached the top of her head. Her huge head, so laden with life. So broad, I could put two mugs of coffee there. I asked Linda if guide dogs could balance cups on their heads. She said it wasn't part of the training.

Soon we would arrive in the city.

Chapter Seven

"Your job," said Kylie, "is to harness your dogs and walk several blocks of Mamaroneck Avenue. It's the main commercial street in the heart of White Plains."

It would be six blocks up, six blocks back. A trainer would always be a half block behind us. Additional trainers would be stationed at street corners. There'd be lots of eyes on us. "You might feel alone," Linda said, but we'd be watched by "pros." It occurred to me I'd never been watched by "pros." I didn't play sports as a kid. I hadn't been coached in movement of any kind. Now I had a circle of canine-vision, walking masters.

* * *

Sometimes I play a mind game called "is it early or too late for different humans"—I try to imagine how much of life's sweetness remains inside people. It's a game of admiration. When I meet old acquaintances after years I can see some have managed to keep their joy.

They still have the "early" within them. You can play the game with anyone—eyeing strangers on a bus, sitting at a concert.

The dogs had "early." The trainers too.

We climbed from the van. Our dogs shook from side to side, greeting each other and their new surroundings.

The morning waited.

* * *

I wasn't the first to go walking. I had to wait in a lounge with a cup of coffee and my notebook. I wrote some lines from memory:

Journal, March 3, 1994:

"Be willing to be a beginner every single morning." (Meis-ter Eckhart)

"Afoot and lighthearted I take to the open road, healthy, free, the world before me." (Walt Whitman)

"You know, it's quite a job starting to love somebody. You have to have energy, generosity, blindness. There is even a moment, in the very beginning, when you have to jump across a precipice: if you think about it you don't do it." (Jean-Paul Sartre)

* * *

Then Kylie came and said it was my turn. Our turn.

It was Corky's moment. She'd show me what she could do.

I'd show her I wasn't afraid.

There is even a moment, in the very beginning, when you have to jump across a precipice . . .

We hurried past storefronts. Corky pulled and I concentrated on my breathing, trying to stay loose. My arm was straight, my shoulders squared, my posture upright. In lecture it had sounded so easy, but now I was moving very fast. I was scared and joyous. Kylie was behind us, monitoring. We were "stepping out," as they say in guide-dog work. Corky was going so swiftly I didn't have time to worry about oncoming shadows—people, street signs—whatever they were, they just dropped behind us.

I'd always been a tippy-toe walker. Now I was putting everything into my feet and for the first time I felt vital in relation to my footfalls. It was a circumstance for which I had no prior lingo: a dog-driven invitation to living full forward. Racing up the sidewalk we were forwardness itself.

Then Corky hit the brakes. Firmly. She'd arrived at our first curb. "God," I thought, "she's doing what the trainers said she'd do." Then she backed up slightly. The harness, the well-known guide-dog accoutrement, is perfectly rigid. Its handle is a steel fork with a skin of leather. As your dog moves you move.

I felt safe at the curb. "Earth will be safe," said the the Buddhist teacher Thich Nhat Hanh, "when we feel in us enough safety."

"Nice stop," said Barbara, a trainer stationed just a few feet away. "That's our Corky girl!"

"And she'll always do that?" I said—it was half a question, half an exclamation.

"Yep," said Barbara. "She'll always do that."

Block two came next.

We stepped out again.

Corky guided, watching, looking a block ahead.

"Man," I thought, "I could let go of all my panic. All my fight-or-flee guesswork walks might just be a thing of the past."

Corky's harness jingled. Her harness actually jingled!

A man called out: "That's a great-looking dog! And you look pretty good too!"

"Thanks," I said, "so do you!" I was feeling good, and more than a little proud.

* * *

We walked another block.

Again Corky came to a stop. We were at the corner of Mamaroneck Avenue and Martine, a tough intersection. Urban. Lots of cars. Metro New York drivers. It certainly wasn't Ithaca. It was all a blur of motion to me.

Corky tracked movement like a predator. I felt her shoulders sway as she looked from side to side. Dogs track movement better than people and have a wider visual field. A Labrador retriever sees 250 degrees while staring straight ahead. A human being sees only 180.

Without turning her head a dog can see a car with her peripheral vision, even if it's still a block away. She sees fields of action. It's a dog's version of Cubism, a Cubist cartoon—each zone filled with activity. Standing on the corner of Mamaroneck and Martine I imagined what Corky might be seeing. As I listened she saw a skateboarder weaving from 85 degrees right. From our left she saw a taxi encroaching the crosswalk and ready to accelerate. In the middle distance, on the far side of the street, a man with a hot dog stand struggled to raise an umbrella. Far off, one hundred yards away, she saw a motorized street-sweeping machine churning up dust.

"Listen to the traffic going with you," said Barbara, who was just behind us. I'd forgotten she was there. I liked the fact she was nearby but wasn't intrusive. Then the traffic began flowing and it was our turn to cross.

I commanded Corky forward. Most people think guide dogs are responsible for deciding when to cross the street, but it's not true. The dog watches traffic. This is why she differs from a family pet. Guide dogs possess a trait called "intelligent disobedience." A blind person hears traffic and decides when to cross the street but a guide won't budge if her handler has made a bad choice. She may in fact back up. So when you enter the crosswalk you can count on a safe crossing.

I said "forward" and we entered the no-man's-land of a crosswalk where a line of impatient cars emitted exhaust. Corky zipped. Before I could think, we were at the far curb. As I found the sidewalk with my foot, Barbara reminded me to praise her. I was so wrapped in wonder I was forgetting to say "Good dog."

"Love her up," said Barbara. Though it wasn't in the

lesson plan, I dropped to my knees and hugged my big yellow ox-headed Labrador girl and told her she was the best thing ever. Then I laughed because I was neither here nor there—not the old blind guy, and not quite the new—but I was happy. Phase one of trust—laughing . . .

Chapter Eight

Safely back in our room I thought about confident walking and wrote in my notebook. I'd felt the power of Corky's authority. She owned the street. I wondered what this might mean for me. Could her poise, her very speed, become, ironically, the key to outstepping a lot of bad thinking? One of the trainers said: "An advantage to the guide dog is you can stop trying to use your limited vision. You can actually walk with your eyes shut." Corky knew lots about it. She nuzzled my arm with her cold nose and I put away my notebook and got down on the floor and held her tightly.

* * *

We embarked on another outing the following morning. We crossed the busy streets of White Plains during rush hour. I made directional choices. I knew where we were going. Boy does a dog appreciate that! "Corky, right," I'd say, and we'd turn, her tail wagging. "She's happy," I thought, "because I can do my part and relieve her of uncertainty. She's got enough on her mind. Knowing our destination—that's my job. Balance. I have something to give."

In turn she got us places. Looking into the distance she made decisions. She angled right anticipating an approaching woman jogging with a stroller. Corky pulled right gently, knowing how to avoid a collision many yards in advance. Corky saw joggers and walkers as clueless creatures. All pedestrians were disarming. She kept tabs on them. I was her beneficiary.

In college I once jotted down a sentiment by Helen Keller: *Optimism is the faith that leads to achievement. Nothing can be done without hope and confidence.* I'd copied her lines because I was uncertain about their accuracy. I thought Keller was a version of Pollyanna. Now I saw I'd failed to recognize how hope and conviction are like a map's coordinates. *Helen Keller, Cartographer*, I wrote in my notebook during "down time" between walks.

* * *

There are many values associated with guide-dog training. The pursuit of peaceful steps is one of them. Corky day by day took me into new realms of footing.

This "peace walking breakthrough" is central to working with a guide. You learn how to read your dog's confidence. And when everything works, your footfalls become peaceful. You say, "Good dog, good dog," and inside you're saying, "Good feet, good us."

Somewhere around day six Linda said: "Corky's turning over to you! She's your girl now!"

She meant we were a team.

* * *

That night I sat up late with students in the coffee lounge. I was interested in what the longtime guide-dog users had to say about life with dogs.

Joseph had been a guide-dog user since the early sixties. He'd had a successful career in insurance. Now he was retired. He was training with "Tinsel," a female chocolate Labrador who he said he was going to call "Tinny."

Although Joseph was completely blind he said he always knew when his dogs were watching him. "A dog's eyes speak," he said. "It's like a light beam or something. And it makes you feel good."

Harriet, who was from Brooklyn and training with her third dog, said, "It's more than just their eyes—I always feel my dog is interested in me. Even when I'm not interesting my dog thinks I'm the best companion."

"You never know how interesting you are," said Aaron. He was from Mississippi and generally reserved. "I mean," he said, "when you open a window, you're a magician for your dog."

"Yes," said Tina, who was getting her second dog. "We're lovable in the ordinary."

I confessed: "It's been just a week for me with Corky, and I don't know quite how to say this—but I've never felt so fast on my feet. Does that feeling stick? Will I always feel like I'm flying?"

"Oh yeah," said Joseph. "Every day."

"It's so much quicker than cane travel, it's not funny," said Aaron.

"I hate cane travel," said Tina. "It's just endless guesswork."

I thought I knew what she was getting at but I asked her to say more.

"Well," she said, "you sweep the cane back and forth and basically you hope you'll find obstacles before colliding with them. It's really primitive."

"With your dog," she said, "the whole thing is fluid because she sees things and adjusts without breaking stride. And when I walk with my sighted friends, I'm always faster than they are. Sighted people can't keep up."

"Sighted people are incredibly primitive," said Aaron.

"Ain't that the truth," said Joseph. They laughed.

"So what do you mean? How are sighted people primitive?" I asked.

Aaron was working on a PhD in languages. He'd been silent for the first few days. But now he was warming up.

"So," he said. "You're in a restaurant and twelve other folks, strangers all, are eyeing you because you're significantly different. Sighted people enjoy novelty and you're the novelty du jour. Even if you're just chewing a muffin, you're entertainment. And then a stranger can't resist and approaches and says: "'I knew a blind person once . . .'"

"Oh God, yeah," said Tina.

"There's some nuance to this," said Aaron. "The stranger once knew a blind guy in college, or a blind person who lived down the street. Sometimes he'll ask if I actually know the aforementioned blind person because, after all, shouldn't all blind people know one another?"

"You're swallowing the damned muffin and you

think, 'What if I asked if he knows all businessmen who wear London Fog raincoats'?

"Now you're in a fix," said Aaron. "The stranger's invitation to chat is also a signal to you, the blind one, to say moderately inspirational things. Or in turn the stranger says upbeat things like: 'I knew a blind guy once who could take apart a radio and put it back together.'"

Aaron continued: "He knew a blind guy who climbed a mountain. He knew a blind guy who went skydiving. Who caught more fish than the rest of them combined . . .

"And you want to say—I knew a short guy once. I knew a short guy who could reach the peanut butter on a shelf with a special device called a stepladder. He was amazing."

"Faux disability heroism," I thought, "is like every other kind of American hero worship. If 'one size fits all' is the United States' universal motto, then surely any distinguishing quality makes a man or woman remarkable. *I knew a guy who could eat more hot dogs than anyone in Peoria. I knew a woman who ate spiders to amuse her children.* In the United States anyone curious is refreshing." I didn't say this. I heard their proper frustration.

"Can't a blind person just be customary?" I thought. Judging by what Aaron had to say, the answer was no.

"I don't put down stray sighted people who ask me dumb questions," Aaron continued. "It is better to be polite. Sometimes I use my dog as a ploy and say: 'I've got to go. The dog needs to take a piss.'

"Anyway," said Aaron, "I don't talk about blindness. There are agencies for that. I tell people I want to talk about neutrinos."

"One thing's certain," said Harriet, who'd been listening and combing her dog. "You're a celebrity with a guide dog. People always approach you."

"Well, I'm not sure I'll mind that," I said, then added, "I like the small, sensible faces of life."

No one knew precisely what to say to that. There was a brief silence. Then Aaron said, "Well you're a poet. But don't let strangers talk you to death!"

Listening to them I wondered if I'd have a problem with strangers. My principle hang-up had always concerned accomplishment—a misunderstanding of accomplishment—as if blindness was an obstacle to success. I'd lived without any examples of blind triumph. Now triumph was all around me. The other students were skilled at living with their disability. Maybe

Aaron didn't like talking with intrusive people, but he was in the world and could live as he wished. I resolved not to care too much about curious strangers. In a way, questions might be a relief after living for so long with blindness as a largely unspoken element of my life.

Chapter Nine

Back again in White Plains we made our way toward Macy's department store. The goal each day was to go someplace new, and a store would present us with our first opportunity to try revolving doors and escalators.

I was feeling dog-man confidence. And that's when Miss Corky leapt backwards, taking me with her. A Jeep had jumped the curb. I tasted my heart for a second. A woman said, "Are you okay? Are you?" Two men talked at once. "Just like that! The dog jumped just like that!" The other said, "I didn't get his license number." And Kylie appeared. She said, "That's what Corky gets paid to do!" Then she said: "We call that in guide-dog work *a traffic check.*"

For Corky this was a routine matter, and Kylie's satisfaction meant we were a success. We continued on our way.

"Oh Corky, good girl, my sweet duck! My precious goose!" I said.

"You're pretty weird," Kylie said.

"Yeah," I said.

As we walked the next block I realized, paraphrasing the poet Theodore Roethke, we'd learn by going where we have to go, but we'd also learn by stopping.

"Intelligent disobedience isn't empathy," said Kylie when I talked to her at the next curb. "It's instinct."

* * *

"Dogs," she said, "have multiple smarts."

We arrived at the entrance of Macy's and a woman asked what my dog's name was.

"Smarty Pants," I said. "But I call her 'Smarty.'"

"That *was* good," said Kylie.

"What was?" I asked.

"Giving that woman a false name. In general you don't want strangers calling your dog's name when you're working her—they'll just start talking to her and distracting her. If you say her name is Smarty they'll call her that and she'll never respond."

"Good to know," I said.

* * *

Back in the training lounge, drinking coffee, I wrote some more about trust in my notebook:

Journal, March 9, 1994:

Don't know why I'm thinking of this now . . . but when I was studying in Helsinki on a Fulbright, 11 years ago, I broke my typewriter. And I took it to a repair shop. I spoke to the proprietor in my mediocre brand of Finnish—typing machine broken . . . can you fix? And then the strangeness of the enterprise came over me, for the typewriter man was deaf and he wrote his responses on a tiny pad of paper. I couldn't read his writing. So I handed him my terrible thick glasses. Ah! He saw the problem. Then he said: "Yes, yes . . ."

Deaf man, blind man, broken machine . . . and mutual trust . . . seeing each other . . . I'll never forget the warmth of that little shop. Old man, inky machines, unspoken kindness . . .

I think dog life will be something like that— communicative, fully understanding, and never with the proper words . . .

* * *

After a long day of walking, we sat alone in our room. With Corky I felt the margins of my loneliness were porous.

I felt the irony of being middle-aged and just beginning to appreciate the richness of being human. Formerly I'd relied on poetry alone to grant me hints about whatever we mean by "life," and now I was feeling all my own joy and melancholy flowing together.

Corky allowed me to put my weak eyes against her face. I tugged gently on her ears. Their softness was like down. "Oh Girlie," I said, "Your ears are supreme. Did you pay extra for those or did they come standard?" I kissed her nose.

Then I lay on the floor and played dead. She came and stood over me and washed my face, her tongue like a silk fish, and then, tiring of the game, she put a paw on my forehead, gently, very gently, as if to say, "Arise." And I laughed, in part because of her gentleness—because there was intelligence in her gesture.

Empathy, at its core, is knowing how not to hurt each other.

I held her paw in my hand and smelled it. It smelled like bread or corn chips—a yeasty odor.

"Corky, how do you stand it, you're perfect!" I said. Then I yawned. And she yawned.

I played a game of contagion with her by pretending to be distressed, waving my arms, shaking all over, saying "Oh, oh, oh!" (Though not too loudly—we were in a dormitory with rather thin walls.)

Corky stood, ran at me, then bounced up and down, eager to be of assistance. Dog researchers call the desire by dogs to help humans "sympathetic concern." "Oh, Corky," I said. "I'm just fooling! What a good girl!"

I knew for the rest of her life I'd need to respect Corky's empathy. And I made a note to myself to never feign distress.

* * *

We walked the grounds of the school at dusk. We were on a path beside a pond. We were loose. "Dogs can't make you feel better about yourself," I thought, "but brisk walking is a reconciliation with whatever isn't you. Walking fast you don't have to ask who you are."

Eventually I stopped and sat on a bench and Corky lay beside me. Soon it would be dinnertime and the students and trainers would gather in the dining hall. It was nice to have a quiet moment, man and Labrador alone in the spring twilight. It was cold and we wouldn't be staying long. But I needed to sit. I was filled with changes—transformations both big and small had come over me in just a few short days. I sat with my left hand on Corky's head and breathed in and out slowly. I was mindful of my healing—not because blindness needed a cure, far from it. I was healing from a wounding failure to love my blindness. I was embracing emotions I hadn't known were in me. Where before I'd felt abandoned, I now appreciated the acceptance of others. Strangers on the streets admired the man-dog walking with our two heads up. Where before I'd experienced the intimidating quality of unseeable spaces, I was feeling some kind of affectionate awareness—an appreciation of what? Of the world's attraction, both spiritually and intellectually. No I didn't need to be cured of disability. Yes, I could open my breathing. I could breathe from deep down, like an opera singer. I could breathe slowly. I could let jubilations into my life—our life, the Corky-Steve life. Sitting on the bench at dusk I felt liberated and a little daffy. "Which is a dog feeling," I thought. Corky looked at me then and wagged her tail.

Chapter Ten

In the lounge I found some books on tape about guide dogs. I knew a little bit about their history but reading more on the subject was captivating. I learned that half-way through the First World War a German physician, Dr. Gerhard Stalling, introduced a blind veteran to his pet dog. The two men were in a hospital garden when Stalling was suddenly called away. When he came back the soldier, whose name is now lost, was laughing as the dog licked his hands. Stalling had a breakthrough. Dogs had been performing heroically on the battlefield. It seemed as though dogs could do almost anything under difficult circumstances. Stalling believed dogs might be trained to guide the blind. The war had produced an astonishing number of blind veterans. The total number of wounded from the First World War remains unknown but during the four and a half years of the conflict 230 soldiers died every hour. Eleven percent of France's entire population was killed. The ten-month Battle of Verdun in 1916 caused over a million casualties. Chlorine and mustard gas killed nearly 90,000 troops and left 1.25 million men permanently disabled. Blindness was a common result of gas warfare and one of John Singer Sargent's most famous paintings (*Gassed*, 1919) depicts a ragged line of soldiers, their eyes bandaged, all the men walking in a line, each man's hand on the shoulder of the man before him—with two sighted men in the lead. The sky is yellow above a field of corpses.

Trench warfare included working dogs. Germany employed 30,000 dogs in the field and their work was divided according to need. Sentry dogs were used on patrols. They were taught to give warning when a stranger entered a secure area. Scout dogs were also used. Their job was more refined—they accompanied soldiers on reconnaissance and had to keep quiet. They could detect the enemy at a distance of a thousand yards, "scenting" and pointing.

Casualty or "mercy" dogs were trained to find wounded or dying soldiers in the heat of battle. They carried medical supplies on their backs. The wounded could use the supplies if they were able, or they could count on the mercy dog to wait with them as they died.

Dogs also ran long distances across battlefields carrying messages, often during artillery attacks. The heroism of working dogs was well known on all sides. The Germans employed 30,000 dogs during the war. British and French forces had approximately 20,000 dogs in the field.

The guide dog was a direct consequence of war. Because dogs had proven themselves capable of miraculous work under the worst battle conditions ever seen, it was clear to Stalling that war dogs could be trained to help the blind navigate the postwar streets, which were filled with automobiles. With a small group of military dog handlers, Stalling began training dogs for blind soldiers. Old photos show trainers and veterans working with German shepherds, all the men wearing peaked hats and long wool coats. In addition to harnesses, the dogs wore tunics bearing the Red Cross logo—the insignia of the battlefield mercy dog.

Stalling's discovery captured the public's imagination. An official guide-dog school opened in Oldenburg in 1916. The sight of veterans and dogs working in traffic was powerful and seemed natural. In the popular imagination blind people had always been accompanied by dogs: a first-century mural in the Roman city of Herculaneum depicts a blind man with his dog. A nineteenth-century woodcut from the United States shows a blind man from Boston being led by a dog and crossing the Commons. Such pairings were likely the products of serendipity—the blind and their dogs forged relationships by necessity. The history of blindness is filled with sorrow. Before reforms like social security and organized rehabilitation services in the twentieth century, the blind often begged for food and shelter—some played musical instruments—many wandered searching for compassion. Dogs helped ease their loneliness and offered untrained navigational assistance.

The war dogs displayed something new, a steadfastness and resilience never fully seen before. Stalling's sense that dogs could work with the blind was both shrewd and far-reaching: the blind would go wherever the public went since dogs were adept at handling the pressures of modern traffic. Motor cars and backfiring trucks were minor annoyances compared to artillery shells.

* * *

The first guide-dog trainers had to teach dogs how to "pull out" and show them their role as navigators. Obstacle courses were devised with sawhorses and logs and low-hanging branches. As they worked, dogs learned they couldn't count on their handlers to make intelligent navigational choices. They also learned to think about the combined width of a man-dog team when walking. A German scientist named Jakob von Uexküll Brull actually developed a rolling cart to replicate the height of a man and the width of a dog team. Dogs pulled these carts and learned to make good street decisions prior to being paired with a blind person. While this method of training is no longer in use, it showcases the creativity of early German training methods.

I started to notice how many of the trainers were "outside the box" people. Not a single one would trade their day job for life in a bank. Conversely no banker would submit to wearing a blindfold for weeks and walking with a dog.

"There's a swashbuckling quality to the guide-dog biz," I thought.

In the foyer where students often waited to board the vans, I found Linda putting neatsfoot oil on leather dog leashes and asked her about the earthy cowboy aspect of guide-dog trainers. How far back did this go?

"In the old days," said Linda, "a trainer named J. P. used to keep his horse out behind the kennels. One day the dogs got loose and he leapt on his steed and took off after them. J. P. always wore tall rubber boots and cable-knit sweaters and he was unkempt and you have to picture suburban people standing on their lawns with their children, waiting for the school bus, and this wild man, a guy who looked almost feral, went pounding down the street on a chestnut stallion chasing a pack of dogs."

"Working with animals has its perks," I said.

"Well, no two days are exactly alike," Linda said. Then she added, "But that's what makes working with animals and people so appealing. Every day is a frontier."

* * *

One night I joined a half-dozen students in the lounge to watch a film, *Love Leads the Way*. It told the story of Morris Frank, the first guide-dog user in the United States. As we settled our dogs beside us and passed a bowl of popcorn, trainer L read the synopsis. Released in 1984 as a made-for-TV movie, it told the story of Frank and his dog, Buddy. It also highlighted Frank's single-handed fight to gain acceptance for guide dogs in America. It dawned on me as I listened to L, the guide dog "as concept" was only sixty-five years old in the United States and Frank was, in historical terms, still nearly our contemporary.

Morris Frank was born in Nashville, Tennessee, to prosperous parents. His mother was blind, and as a boy he served as her sighted guide. Frank's own blindness occurred as a direct consequence of accidents. When he was six he went blind in one eye after being struck by a branch while riding a horse. At sixteen he was blinded in his other eye while boxing with a friend. Strangely, his mother's blindness also involved improbable events: she'd gone blind in one eye when giving birth to her first child; then she lost the vision in her remaining eye when she was thrown by a horse. These calamities happened during and just after WWI when ophthalmology was still primitive in the United States.

Despite his blindness Morris Frank attended Vanderbilt University and supported himself by tuning pianos and selling insurance. In 1927, when he was nineteen, he read an article by a wealthy American heiress named Dorothy Eustis in the popular magazine *The Saturday Evening Post*. Eustis was a fancier of the German shepherd and was leading an expatriate's life in Switzerland, where she was working to restore the shepherd to its former glory as a solid working dog. By the late 1920s many American and European dog breeders believed the shepherd was in decline owing to overbreeding.

As she traveled through Europe in search of breeding stock, Eustis visited Germany, where she encountered guide dogs. Her article in *The Saturday Evening Post* gave Americans their first glimpse of dogs for the blind. Her prose is now terribly dated but it reflects the common feeling in the late nineteen-twenties that blindness was a great misfortune. She wrote:

"To everyone, I think, there is always something particularly pathetic about a blind man . . . His other senses may rally to his aid, but they cannot replace his eyesight. To man's never-failing friend has been accorded this special privilege. Gentlemen, I give you the German Shepherd dog."

* * *

In 1927 there was no systematic means of training blind people in how to travel. Almost no one knew how to help Morris Frank. The opening scenes of *Love Leads the Way* show Frank struggling unsuccessfully with a cane, bumping into strangers, nearly helpless on Nashville's sidewalks.

Accordingly Eustis's article offered Frank some hope—Europeans were training dogs and blind people to move safely and independently, and perhaps best of all, with dignity. Frank wrote to Eustis: "Is what you say really true? If so, I want one of those dogs! And I am not alone. Frank added: "Thousands of blind like me abhor being dependent on others. Help me and I will help them. Train me and I will bring back my dog and show people here how a blind man can be absolutely on his own. We can then set up an instruction center in this country to give all those here who want it a chance at a new life."

Eustis called Frank and invited him to Fortunate Fields, her dog-training school in Switzerland.

He replied: "Mrs. Eustis, to get my independence back, I'd go to hell."

* * *

I was captivated by the film. Frank met his dog, Buddy, and learned to trust not only his dog but a team of people. Eustis assigned a dog trainer named Jack Humphrey to train Buddy and in turn train Frank. Humphrey worked the team hard.

Every scene in the film offered a vignette of "firsts"— returning to New York, Frank was met by reporters who didn't believe a dog could guide a blind person. Together Buddy and Frank crossed West End Avenue, at the time one of New York's busiest streets, and with that feat, the guide dog "arrived" in America, both as a fact, and as a figure that effectively captured the public's imagination.

Frank was as good as his word, and with Dorothy Eustis's help, he founded the first guide-dog school in the United States—The Seeing Eye—in 1929. They started the program in Nashville, then moved it to Morristown, New Jersey, where it remains today.

When the film was over I needed to know more about Morris Frank. Luckily, Guiding Eyes had a taped copy of Frank's 1957 book *The First Lady of the Seeing Eye* in its library and I listened to it rather religiously between training walks.

Though I'd been reluctant to admit my blindness, or at least to say I needed help, and had been slow to get a guide dog, I'd always imagined dogs for the blind were a part of the natural order. I'd never thought about dogs and blindness and civil rights. But as I learned more about Morris Frank's history, I found that his freedom of mobility with Buddy was blocked in many places.

Before he left Switzerland, Dorothy Eustis forewarned him that being the first guide-dog user in America would require tremendous persistence and poise. According to Frank she told him: ". . . you must not forget that signs saying 'No Dogs Allowed' are almost everywhere—in restaurants, hotels, office buildings, and stores. If the blind man's dog can't be with him in the places he has to go, of what value is it to him? And what about restrictions on trains, streetcars, and busses? If a person can't use his dog to get to work, it's obvious he can't hold down a job. How will it ever be possible for the organization to succeed unless the guide dogs are welcome in all public places?"

At home in Tennessee Frank saw what Eustis meant: many businesses wouldn't let his guide dog in. He was refused transport by buses and trains. For the rest of his life he fought for the right to travel where the public goes—a fight guide-dog users ultimately won with persistence and the exemplary behavior of their dogs. By the 1960s the public accepted guides as professional animals, understanding they weren't the sloppy pets many business owners initially declared them to be.

* * *

I thought of Morris Frank during our remaining days at Guiding Eyes. We learned how to tuck our dogs under chairs; how to give leash corrections to keep them "on task." We practiced "daily obedience" by having them sit, stay, and lie down, then come to us. They were trained to heel when we were standing and to sit when we needed them to sit. Our dogs had manners. We learned that like Morris Frank we'd be ambassadors for the guide-dog movement, that it was important for each of us to become a superior dog handler. Henceforth, every time we'd enter a supermarket or restaurant or ride on a train—we needed to think like Morris Frank. I was keenly impressed by this. I felt the honor of being a small part of guide-dog tradition.

*　　*　　*

On day seven the whole class went to a local supermarket. I hadn't realized how tricky this would be when Linda announced the exercise. The plan was for us to work through the crowded aisles. Corky and I entered the A&P through the familiar electric door and proceeded to walk among mountains of oranges. We walked rather deftly through an intersection of pineapples and packaged roses and then we hit the cheese section where Corky was literally stunned by the fragrances of Asiago and blue, Gruyère and Parmesan. I don't know which cheese stopped her in her tracks—maybe the

Fontina with its odor of honey and mushrooms—but she hit the brakes, raised her head, and scented deeply. She stopped so fast I ran into her and stumbled slightly. Corky was stupefied. I wondered if Morris Frank had a moment like this. The heroic guide dog and man, clobbered by Brie and Camembert. I asked myself: "What would Morris Frank do?"

"Tell her to hup up," said Linda, who was behind me. "Yes," I thought, "that's just what Morris Frank would have done."

"Hup up," I said, and gave Corky a quick leash correction. We were off again, heading toward the seafood department.

She sailed through the store, avoiding shopping carts and towering displays of cereal. We walked without distraction beside an open refrigerator case filled with steaks and lamb chops. "Good girl," I said. "Good girl."

* * *

In the evening lecture Kylie said: "One thing you will discover when you get home is that going places with a guide dog is like being a movie star." I heard Aaron laugh.

"Wherever you go, you'll be the main focus of public attention."

Linda joined in: "It's funny to think about, but there aren't very many guide dog teams in the United States. There are approximately ten thousand. This means most people have never seen a guide dog. So it also means you're an emissary."

Kylie said, "Though your dog is trained to go everywhere—planes, trains, and escalators—you'll meet airline personnel who've never seen a working dog. Hotel clerks. Waiters. Cab drivers."

Kylie continued: "As trainers we encounter this all the time. At movie theaters; shopping malls; at Grand Central Station—people say, 'Is that a guide dog? I've never seen one before.'

"So you and your dog really are celebrities," she said. "And you're true ambassadors whether you like it or not."

"This means you can't let your dog eat off the floor in a restaurant; can't feed her French fries," said Linda.

"When dining out, your dog must always be tucked safely under a table where people can't step on her," she added.

"And no matter where you are, you need to have

control of her," said Linda. "Service animals are allowed everywhere but the biggest rule, the 'supreme directive,' is that your dog must always be under your control."

Again I thought of Frank. I remembered Dorothy Eustis telling him his dog would always have to be under control and that his second challenge upon returning to America (after fighting his way into public places) would be to demonstrate a guide dog was no more fuss than a cane.

In the days to come as we worked in more and more public spaces this would be our focus. We'd be tracing Morris Frank's journey all the way to the end.

Chapter Eleven

I was in great spirits—even a bit merry. I felt it from the instant I woke. I felt it all day. It wasn't just simple contentment.

I was working, sweating, half running in traffic, giving Corky all my heart, every ounce. Over midmorning coffee Kylie told me she'd never meant to be a dog trainer. "I was planning on graduate school in sociology," she said. "Anyway, one day I was in downtown White Plains in a savings bank. I was cashing a check. And out the window I saw three or four guide dogs going by with blind people—or maybe they were trainers—I didn't know. But the sight really pulled me, I mean it took me over. I could really see myself with the blind and guide dogs. It was as if I'd been waiting for that moment."

She laughed. "Looking back on it, grad school would have been easier.

"I'd no idea how hard the work would be.

"For one thing," she said, "becoming a guide-dog

trainer is an apprentice process like a Renaissance guild. You study with a senior trainer, who's like an artist.

"Being an apprentice trainer starts out hard because you're in the kennel," she said. "It's much worse than mixing colors for Michelangelo, because you shovel dog poop, lug fifty-pound sacks of food, real grunt work.

"You don't get to the training part of the job until you've proven your mettle," she said.

"How long does that take?" I asked.

"Sometimes two or three years," she said. "But you know it's not all in the kennel. We get to follow what's going on in classes, assist the students, follow guide-dog teams. We live in the dorm and wear blindfolds for an extended time just so we can better appreciate the daily, hourly, even minute-by-minute experience of navigating without sight. We learn a lot."

* * *

There really was a lot to learn.

It seemed sometimes there were a hundred techniques to this dog business. We learned how to enter and pass through revolving doors. Corky went on the outside—the larger side of the moving cubicle—and I learned to guard her tail from being pinched. We practiced this several times, my lovely dog in agreement, over and over again through the spinning wicket. We took baby steps, inching our way ahead, pushing the door slowly. "These will soon be replaced by wheelchair-friendly doors because of the Americans with Disabilities Act," said Linda. "But you need to know how to do this in case you find yourself someplace where this is the only type of door."

"Here's to alternative doors," I thought. "Who invented the revolving door?" I wondered. "Some torturer—maybe the same guy who conceived of the iron maiden." Later I actually looked it up; the revolving door was invented in 1888 by Theophilus Van Kannel, a Philadelphia inventor, who is reputed to have had a phobia of opening conventional doors, especially for women. Go figure. In any case, I resolved to avoid the damned things wherever I could.

Every day in training was a classic ballroom dance: turning, feeling with hands and toes, turning again, leading Corky, being led by her, all to the rhythms of whispering cars.

I learned that Corky would curl up tight on the floor of a car, right beneath the glove compartment in the front seat. We practiced the maneuver, man and dog, in and out of a sedan. I stepped part way in with my left leg and called her. She climbed in delicately and lay down. Then I sat, pulling my right leg in. It was cramped and awkward. I'd need to learn some yoga. But Corky could ride this way if we had to. And I knew how to accomplish her positioning. Guide-dog work was all about the accomplishment of daily techniques, all of them necessary if you're taking a dog everywhere.

* * *

The techniques of working with a dog were about safety, companionship, and looking out for each other. This was easy to say but harder to put into action. My mind was occupied with details: how to put the harness on and take it off without smacking Corky in the face; how to adjust her belly strap so she'd be comfortable; how to put on her training collar—it was trickier than it sounds—if the collar was backwards you couldn't give your dog a leash correction. One had to learn how to feel for the chain as it passed through the rings. If the chain met the ring at the bottom it was incorrectly positioned. Off with the collar, on with the collar, Corky sat, her face reflecting concern. Good old Empathy Dog. Worried about her owner's efforts. I imagined her thinking: "I want my man to look better than the other students." But I wasn't better than the others. I put her collar on, took it off, and saw I was only batting 500. I felt inept, and resolved when alone to practice by putting Corky's collar over my wrist. It was tricky all right, but not as hard as cleaning her ears. We were instructed how to reach deep into our dogs' ear canals with cotton pads. We were given bottles of Otic Cleanser and we learned how to apply it. We learned how to brush our dogs' teeth with chicken-flavored toothpaste. We were given heartworm prevention tablets and flea-and-tick repellent. They gave us a brush and comb; a set of aluminum dog dishes. All I could think was, "How am I going to fit this stuff in my tiny suitcase?"

Chapter Twelve

Day eighteen and it was time to go to New York City. Kylie noted the trip was a choice. "Some students really want to go to Manhattan with their dogs, and some don't," she said. It was up to us. Tina and Aaron elected to stay behind. "Been there and done that," Aaron said.

In my junior year of college I'd wanted desperately to travel to Manhattan to hear a renowned poet read his work at the 92nd Street Y. But I had no one to accompany me. I stayed home in Geneva and listened to Billie Holiday records and in the manner of young people, felt my deprivation bitterly. I could have taken the Greyhound bus, but what then? How would I walk alone? How would I manage the subway? The world had been beyond my reach. Now going to New York with a dog, a powerful dog, seemed like something out of a superhero comic. As our train moved beside the Hudson River I stroked Corky's silky ears and then, softly, I began to cry. I'd spent my adult life living as a pallid child. And fearful. But with my dog, the mill wheel of progress was turning inside me. I was poised to walk New York City, to learn it—to learn I could do it. A woman across the aisle asked if I was okay. I told her I was fine, that I was about to be free.

*　*　*

Many people think New York must be a tough place for the blind, but in truth once you've had training with a white cane or a dog, it's a great place. The layout of its avenues and streets forms a grid which makes knowing your location rather simple. Though the sidewalks are crowded and the traffic is intense, New Yorkers are helpful, perhaps because so many come from someplace else, and when you ask questions on a street corner strangers are kind. Walking from the train with Corky and entering the main concourse of Grand Central was like a dream—we moved among throngs of commuters, zipping around clusters of people reading signs. In the majesty of the railway palace we stopped too. I wanted to take it all in. Our trainer Linda was behind us, watching. A stray passenger asked if I needed directions. "No," I said, "I'm just absorbing the glory of this place!" As I stood there two other people approached wanting to help. "This is a New York I didn't know

existed," I thought. It's the New York a guide dog at-
tracts. "Nice dog," said the second man who wanted to
point me in the right direction. We headed toward the
Forty-Second Street exit. Corky was delighted. Her tail
thumped against my leg. She was in her element. I felt it
in our speed. This was no unpleasant test. We were nim-
ble and commanding. We exited the station and entered
a sunny spring day. We were in. Were in New York. I
wanted to cry again but we were walking too fast.

We passed some men playing a curbside card game;
we skirted left and passed a girl with a rolling suitcase.
We stepped around a subway grate, pushed to the curb
at Forty-Second and Vanderbilt. Corky looked left and
right. Two people jaywalked but she didn't budge. A car
accelerated in front of us. I smelled a cigar. I wondered
if it was from the taxi or the far side of the street. Linda
said we were looking good.

*   *   *

Corky was calm but even so, the bustle of Fifth Avenue
overloaded my circuits. It felt as though I'd had a dozen
cups of coffee. Then I had a bizarre experience, a neurological hijacking—a fight-or-flee reflex—and ordered
Corky to cross Forty-Ninth Street though we didn't

"have the light." She looked left and right, saw a gap in the traffic, and took off. We were jay walking like ten million other New Yorkers and though we reached the far side safely, Linda caught up with us and said, "You almost gave me a heart attack. Listen for the traffic flow."

Walking the next few blocks I felt better. My mistake crossing against the light came from energy rather than fear and this was an achievement, failing to be afraid.

We walked up Park Avenue and entered the Waldorf Astoria Hotel. The doorman bade us welcome. He displayed gladness. My "no longer being afraid" meant I could hear notes of optimism. In the past, strange places had often seemed forbidding.

"Welcome to the Waldorf, sir," said the doorman, adding, "What a sharp dog!"

"Thank you," I said.

I remembered to say "Good dog."

We swayed together side by side on the red carpet in the foyer.

There was a general fragrance of lilies.

"We can come to places like this; we can find our way; we're New Yorkers!" I said to Corky, though not loudly.

The rug was soft as a cloud.

There was something august and funereal about the odors of furniture wax and flowers and the odd hush of the place. And as I would do so many times over the coming years I got down on one knee and hugged my dog.

Men and women passed us, headed for the Park Avenue exit.

"Wow," said a woman, seeing us.

I heard the smile in her voice.

I heard an elevator open.

I thought of the history of the place.

I remembered during World War II a train platform was constructed under the Waldorf for President Franklin D. Roosevelt. He could exit the train in privacy—the Secret Service would raise him from his wheelchair and help him into an open sedan. The car would then be lifted to the street in a customized elevator.

I thought of FDR and the stagecraft required to conceal his disability from voters. Well, I'd done that too, though I never had any voters—I just had shadow men and women whom I'd followed, hoping to arrive at my destinations. Jesus, that had taken work. And what a battery drain it had been. Now I was visible with my disability and more pleased about it than I'd ever thought possible. More than pleased—I was loaded with energy.

* * *

That night at Guiding Eyes I talked with classmates about being pleased for the first time with their dogs. Doug recalled walking solo with his first guide dog after returning home. He walked ten blocks from his house to a motorcycle shop and talked about bikes with a sales guy. Then he walked some more and had lunch in a diner. "Nothing," he said, "had ever been that good, no conversation or sandwich had ever matched it." In the condensed version of guide-dog life, all at once everything is reachable. *Reachable* is a word sighted people rarely have to think about—but it's one of the main coordinates of independence.

Doug said when he first hit the street with his dog, "People saw me—like before I got a dog they'd see my white cane and look away, but now they had a point of contact and could say something; even if it was just 'Great dog,' the ice was broken. All of a sudden I was having conversations with strangers. It was like breaking through to the other side of something." Standing in the Waldorf I too felt I'd crossed over to a new kind of living. I was in a public place, a strange spot, and yet I was composed. I was calm because Corky was calm. Dogs reflect us and our moods. A dog's stress hormones rise and fall along with its owner's stress. This is why dogs yawn with us. I was sitting beside Corky in our dorm room and I yawned. She yawned. I saw it made sense. If a man is calm his dog is calm. But why did I feel her calmness on Fifth Avenue? She couldn't have been taking her emotional cues from me.

Like all topflight guide-dog schools, Guiding Eyes breeds its own dogs. Unlike show-dog breeders, guide-dog breeders focus on developing invisible traits. The characteristics they hope to produce in dogs are wide ranging—disposition, confidence, the ability to recover from sudden upsetting experiences—just to name a few. The breeding program also promotes breeding strains that are resistant to diseases and allergies. And as if these qualities aren't enough, they also aim to assure repeatability. They need a steady supply of field-worthy dogs.

One night a trainer named Jack told me a story from the old days when guide-dog schools didn't have breeding programs and relied on donated dogs. Jack had been a trainer for almost fifty years. "We used to go to animal shelters and dog pounds," he said. "We'd look for tough dogs back then, dogs that could stand up to the training. We'd go to the pound and the dogs would be crazy, jumping and carrying on. If they looked us right in the eye we'd take them. It helped if they didn't bite us!

"Those old dogs were tough," he said, and laughed. "Sometimes they really did bite us."

We were in the dining room drinking strong black Chinese tea and rain was coming down hard, hitting the dining-room windows. In a few minutes all the students would come in for dinner. Corky rolled over for a belly rub and I reached down and stroked her.

"In the early fifties, dog training was still based on a military model," said Jack. "We pushed those dogs hard. The training was 'aversive,' which meant each time a dog did the wrong thing it received a heavy correction. The dogs grew to anticipate the correction and would do the right thing. You could say those were the bad old days. And of course we trained all kinds of dogs—Bouviers, boxers, shepherds, Weimaraners, standard poodles, Belgian Tervurens, border collies, and mixed breeds—if a dog was tough and loaded with life we could train it. Trouble was, once we'd trained one of those donated dogs, we couldn't be certain of repeating our success.

We spent way too much time looking for dogs that might make it. And often we had more failures than successes in the early days."

I thought about those early days. Even as late as the 1950s a guide dog was a rare sight. The pressure to produce perfect dogs must have been on the mind of every trainer. "Yeah," said Jack, "we were all ambassadors. And we felt that the large failure rate with found or donated dogs was completely unacceptable. By breeding our own dogs we could assure better and more consistent results."

In the mid 1960s, Helen Ginnel, a champion breeder of Labrador retrievers, donated a large portion of her "Whygin Labradors" breeding colony to Guiding Eyes. "Almost overnight we were in business," said Jack. "We had superior dogs to work with. And lots of them."

He told me how with a breeding program in place they could count on having dogs readily available that would be of medium size, healthy—and they'd be calm, easy to handle by persons with minimal dog-handling skills. They'd also be confident in all environments, able to cope with the pressure of making decisions, and they wouldn't be distracted around other dogs.

Jack explained that "repeatability" was the principal

factor in the adoption of Labradors for guide-dog work in the 1970s.

"We found we could breed confident Labs. They could get on an airplane in New York and arrive in San Francisco and be happy. Suddenly we had dogs who didn't just do the work—they loved the work."

He told me the German shepherd was a superb working dog, but over the years they had trouble producing enough dogs to meet the demands of training. Shepherds could be tense, sometimes nipping at people's ankles. He explained that they still bred shepherds but couldn't turn them out with the same consistency as Labs.

"So, in a way, things haven't changed that much since the days when Dorothy Eustis was trying to restore the German shepherd as a working dog," I said.

"That's true," said Jack. "But it's also true shepherds are herding dogs. When they're in a familiar place they're great guide dogs, but in strange locations they can become agitated. And finding shepherds that don't have these traits is harder than it is with Labs."

"Why do you still breed shepherds at all?" I asked.

"Because a great shepherd is a first-rate guide. And many guide-dog users who began with German shepherds still want one. Our problem has to do with assuring solid guide dogs are always in the pipeline. Trainers need dogs to train. Clients need dogs when they need them—and our Labradors are a 'get up and go' solution. But when we have a great shepherd we know we have a quality guide dog."

He went on to explain the calmness factor.

He told me how guide-dog success is multifaceted. On one side there's the breeding program. They breed dogs for temperament and health. They want dogs that are outgoing, eager, self-assured, and readily able to problem solve. They want dogs with "recoverability"— it's okay for them to be surprised by a sudden noise or strange sight, but they prize the dogs that can't be surprised twice.

"We want dogs that say, 'Been there, done that, no big deal,'" said Jack.

"So temperament is the first side."

We poured more hot water into our cups. The tea was good.

"Another side has to do with nurture," said Jack. "Our puppies receive love from volunteer families. Never underestimate loving-kindness. Behind every confident dog is a team of loving people."

I'd never thought about puppy raising as an act of love. It was almost overpowering. There I was, in love with Corky, and Jack was telling me there was a transmission of love behind this.

Jack said puppy raisers are the foundation. They're responsible for the successful upbringing of the dogs. But they aren't called upon to introduce the dogs to traffic. They do teach the dogs verbal signals and hand signals.

"When you become a puppy raiser," Jack said, "you really stretch your spirit."

"We teach our puppy raisers that the handler and the dog must maintain awareness of each other at all times when they're together," he said. "Either handler or dog may be engaged in something else while still maintaining awareness. Awareness is demonstrated by response to a change in the other. For instance, the handler should notice if a dog moves or changes focus; the dog notices if the handler moves or alters his actions."

"Does this eventually become natural?" I asked.

"Exactly. Mutual awareness becomes a way of life," said Jack. "And when a puppy grows up and comes back for its adult training—its guide-dog education—the dog will focus 'right in' on his or her person."

"What other kinds of things do the puppy raisers need to know?" I asked.

"Tons of things," said Jack. "Body language. When a puppy raiser offers feedback to a dog they need to use their whole body; both voice and actions tell a dog how pleased or displeased you are. Dogs pay attention to everything. You've noticed how Corky watches you? She's watching you as if you were a dancer."

Jack paused for a moment, then said: "You'd be surprised how many people think they understand dogs but can't read them. Dogs look at us for confirmation, or with expectation, or concern, or even with impatience. Our goal is to train each puppy by understanding these 'reads.'

"We're trying to foster confidence," he said. "Your basic pet owner thinks, 'Well I don't understand my dog, I'll give him a hard leash correction.' Our puppy raisers learn to understand everything about a dog. We want each dog's inner poise to come out—like the grain in wood."

I said: "These puppies have better childhoods than I did. When I was a kid no one tried to bring out my inner poise."

"Right," said Jack, "and no one tells us we're part of

something big, a big loving life. Or maybe they do if we're lucky. But every puppy learns this."

"I can feel the confidence when I'm walking with Corky," I said. "She often looks at me, as if to say, 'See what we did!'"

"That," said Jack, "has everything to do with the puppy raisers."

There was a transmission of love behind our triumphs. People had loved Corky and fed her, housed her, laughed with her, and then, when their bond was deepest, they gave her back to the school. The act had a purity about it—a quality one may call rejoicing. I could feel it. I who'd spent my days taking unhappiness too much to heart.

Chapter Thirteen

After three weeks of training, Linda said it was time for graduation. We could invite our parents, friends, family, anyone we wished. As with all commencements, we'd be celebrating human accomplishment; but then again, we'd be honoring our dogs. They'd been through eight months of training and a year of structured life with their raisers. In dog years they'd been to college and graduate school. "This is their ceremony too," Linda said.

Linda continued: "Your puppy raisers are coming. This is a huge day for them. Seeing these successful teams brings them a sense of fulfillment. And these dogs carry a lot of love inside. More than a little has come from the puppy-raising families."

Though Linda didn't say it, it was clear: graduation was about something bigger than each student's individual experience. I worried it might be awkward. This was an old habit, imagining how a scenario would seem to others. I pictured the class in front of a room, all of us wearing wrinkly clothes; each with our dog beside us, all smiling and failing to look directly at the camera. It didn't sound promising. But I'd do it for Corky's puppy raisers. I'd resist embarrassment, at least for an afternoon.

*   *   *

My mother still didn't like my embrace of blindness. Now that graduation was coming I called her to share how good the training experience had been. I talked about Corky, told her how Corky had taken me through the Waldorf. I said she was slowly working her way into my bed at night. "In Corky's world the bed is the sign of justice," I told my mother. Then she said it: "I wish you weren't doing this. Now everyone will know you can't see . . ."

I was never going to change her. And when all was said and done it wasn't my job. My job (so to speak) was to travel with Corky, forgetting old fantasies about mind over matter, to forget my mother's insistence that not thinking about disability would make it vanish.

I let out a long sigh. Sensing preoccupation Corky nuzzled my hand. I knew it was finally time to defeat my mother's idée fixe. My heart would no longer be subdued. I went outdoors and sat on the porch and thought about my blind-dog self, so freshly bold.

Our trainers spoke of "turning over"—the transfer of a guide dog's love to its new owner. "She's turning over to you," was the best pat on the back I'd ever received. There'd been no praise in my life to equal it. "Bring on graduation," I said. I said it for Corky. "Look at us, girl," I said. "Just look! We've turned over!"

I called my sister Carol, four years my junior, now a physician in Manhattan. While I'd struggled to find walking room in the world, Carol had gone far. But like me she knew what a difficult person our mother was. Like me, she'd struggled to find emotional purchase and freedom.

Should I invite our parents to commencement? I asked my sister. I feared our sorrowing mother and ascetic father would ruin the occasion. Carol would be entirely celebratory. "Who doesn't want to see a dog graduate from college?" she said. She said having our parents at the ceremony would be stressful, but it was worth the effort to invite them.

"Maybe they'll learn something," she said.

"You know," she said after a pause, "I've always been worried about you."

"Please be specific," I said, laughing.

"When you're with me in New York, I'm anxious for you," she said. "That's why I'm always grabbing your arm."

"I know," I said.

"It's funny," I said, "but growing up with Mom, I felt like being visually impaired was a kind of stain on the family."

"The only stain on the family," said Carol, "is *The Momster* herself."

"Well you know," I said, "the main thing is she drinks too much. And she never goes anywhere."

"Yeah," said Carol, "which is how she sees your blindness . . . just don't talk about it and don't go out."

"How does Dad live with her?" I asked.

"He reads books and more books," Carol said.

"And the more he keeps his own counsel, the more he doesn't have to think about customary human relations," she said.

"But the whole thing is so improbable," I said. "I mean, if you had a kid who was blind, wouldn't you teach him how to live?"

"Not if you're them," she said. "You remember how it was . . . back in high school . . . you'd come home at three in the afternoon and Mom would be passed out on the sofa with the shades drawn.

"There's your preparation for life," she said.

"Yes," I replied, "but I should have done this sooner—learned how to do things earlier . . ."

"You read books with your one half-sighted eye," she said. "That's what they taught you to do.

"Hey," she said, "it's not so bad . . . not now anyway . . . and I can't wait to meet Miss Corky!"

I invited Carol to visit a week before the ceremony. I felt giddy. I was excited to introduce her to Corky and I danced in my room and Corky followed, jumping up and down. I felt like some weird berserk Viking. I was experiencing raw exuberance and it was utterly uncomplicated. It was Sunday. Carol would arrive around two p.m. It was almost one. I had a blues harp and I played it and whirled around the room while Corky wagged.

That's when it happened—the "it" improbable, unforeseeable, but clear—I entered the life of confident blindness, that thing I'd scarcely been able to imagine. Perhaps I'd never fully imagined it—but suddenly I was in the world as an adept blind guy with a superior dog.

We were twirling around the bed when a knock came at the door. I opened it. Corky pushed her nose into the corridor. There before us stood the mayor of New York City. He was with his wife and children and a photographer and the president of Guiding Eyes. "Hi," said the mayor. "I'm Rudy Giuliani."

Rudy had come to receive a "release dog" for his family. A release dog is just what the name implies— it's a guide dog that didn't make it all the way through training but will make an exceptional family pet. These dogs are highly prized and there's a long waiting list. Many release dogs join police departments or the Bureau of Alcohol, Tobacco, Firearms and Explosives and work as detection dogs.

Rudy wasn't yet "America's Mayor," and he hadn't yet cashed in his political and PR capital as "the man who cleaned up New York," but he was working on it. Instead of his charcoal Armani suit he wore a Members Only aqua baseball jacket and blue jeans.

"Hello, Mr. Mayor," I said. "I'm Steve and this is Miss Corky!"

Corky eyed everyone and displayed good body language, an alert "ho hum."

I was an ambassador—a circumstance Linda had told us would happen and happen frequently.

I shook hands with the mayor's wife and assumed

the pose of a confident guide-dog team, the role first played by Morris Frank. "Of course, Morris Frank would be wearing a suit," I thought, "and I resemble a lunatic from the woods." I had long, uncombed hair, and was wearing a cable-knit sweater covered with dog hair.

* * *

Journal, March 20, 1994:

When a dog is your teacher you find you're the one who's spent his life uneasy in his own skin. You're the one who lived by rote, who never slowed down, and seldom if ever luxuriated in the present. The dog teacher says, as if she's been reading Robert Frost, "I'm pleased. You come too."

* * *

My dear sister understood what a rare opportunity Guiding Eyes represented for me. When she arrived on campus we went to an empty lounge and I let Corky out of her harness, unsnapped her leash, and she ran and stopped, changed direction, ran again, stopped, then zeroed in on Carol's face and gave her a significant wash.

Within half an hour Carol said: "I was surprised to

meet the mayor, but I'd rather be with Corky anytime."
And Corky had flopped on her back and was performing a horizontal hula with all four feet in the air.

Carol wanted to know what I knew just then that I hadn't known before meeting Corky.

"I didn't know what a dog could do," I said.

"What do you mean?" she asked.

"I knew dogs love us and offer us opportunities to love them back," I said, "but I didn't know that dogs will take us in and give us the benefit of their instincts."

I told her how in Manhattan Corky inserted her body between my feet and the gap separating the subway platform and the train.

"I just didn't know this was possible," I said. "We grew up with great pets," I told her. "I loved those dogs, but I'd never have guessed they could extend their deepest inclinations our way."

* * *

After Carol left I wrote in my journal, trying to understand my new "disability/dog" connection:

I like myself better with Corky. Does America's love of dogs help when it comes to being in public with a disability?

Yes. Dogs are icebreakers; they're tribal totems; they trans-form space.

Am I entirely better off because I have a dog? Probably not . . .

Note to self: be careful not to anthropomorphize your dog, not to idealize her. But do acknowledge your trust. Foolish not to.

* * *

We'd only two more days of training.

We visited an agricultural college where we roamed among goats, chickens, donkeys, and sheep. Some of the paths were narrow and we passed within an arm's length of sheep.

Corky was so in tune with her work I finished the course without fully realizing it. We'd walked the gaunt-let of critters without incident.

* * *

We took a night walk in the nearby town of Mount Kisco. The shopping district comprised a clean circle, and we passed the usual cluster of coffee places, delis, electronics shops. The night air was cold and everyone moved fast. I still couldn't get over how swift guide dogs are. "No more cautious night walks for me," I thought. We were really booking.

Every element of guide-dog training has a purpose and the Mount Kisco walk wasn't just a bit of fun. The town was flooded with motorists. It was surprising. Cars were everywhere. It felt like small-town America in the 1950s as drivers circled the downtown over and over. Engines revved. Tires squealed. The whole effect was energizing. I was Jumpin' Jack Flash. It was a gas. We were flying through mist.

* * *

"Out of your vulnerabilities will come your strength," said Freud. As I walked around Mount Kisco I decided that I liked the guy I used to be. The indomitable will of my former self was still a part of my experience. A life of feigned sight hadn't been wasted. I'd learned to listen while stumbling around. It took boldness to travel without help. And now, with fine-tuning, I was a quicker, more refined man of the street.

And Corky? She liked having a partner who could let go of his anxieties.

* * *

The days at Guiding Eyes began to feel like a NASA countdown—three days till graduation, two, one . . .

We had visits with the vet; our dogs were bathed; we learned from a masseuse how to give our dogs massages. We played rock and roll loudly and danced. There's an old Swedish proverb: "Shared joy is a double joy," and we were twelve times double joy. We took our dogs to a fenced yard and let them run. We swapped jokes.

A snake and rabbit collided at an intersection. They immediately began arguing with one another as to who was at fault. When the snake remarked that he'd been blind since birth, and thus should be given additional leeway, the rabbit said that he, too, had been blind since birth. The two animals then forgot about the accident and began commiserating concerning the problems of being blind. The snake said that his greatest regret was the loss of his identity. He'd never been able to see his reflection in the water, and for that reason didn't know exactly what he looked like, or even what he was. The rabbit declared he had the same problem. Seeing a way they could help each other, the rabbit proposed that one feel the other from head to toe, and then try to describe what the other animal was. The snake agreed, and started by winding himself around the rabbit. After a few moments, he announced, "You've got very soft, fuzzy fur, long ears, big rear feet, and a little fuzzy ball for a tail. I think that you must be a bunny rabbit!" The rabbit was much relieved to find his identity, and proceeded to return the favor to the snake. After feeling the snake's body for a few minutes, he asserted, "Well, you're scaly, you're slimy, you've got beady little eyes, you squirm and slither all the time, and you've got a forked tongue. I think you're a lawyer!"

We laughed; sang together with a tuneless guitar; threw tennis balls for our dogs. Group relief had broken out.

Chapter Fourteen

My mother, Evelyn, was a saboteur of family occasions and so she arrived for graduation feeling faint. My sister and I dragged her to the kitchen for orange juice and crackers. She had diabetes, which required attention, but she also had Ménière's disease, a disorder of the inner ear affecting balance. This meant she could fall over at any time. Added to this dire possibility was her stone-faced manner. Sometimes I thought she was just a step shy of having Munchausen by proxy—she seemed to live just to make everyone sick. She swayed and waved her arms.

"Listen," said my father, Allan, who invariably spoke as the ship was sinking, "we'd better take her to your room."

We moved through a celebratory throng of dogs and graduates, families, puppy raisers, trainers, my father and sister holding Evelyn by the arms, Corky and I in front. In the dorm room, alone, with only our clan for company, Evelyn was suddenly restored. She stopped depending to and fro.

Carol, who always called Evelyn "Evy Jo" because her full name was Evelyn Josephine, said: "Listen, Evy, you better sit." And Evelyn sat on the bed and stared balefully like a dowager queen. Then she said: "You go on without me. I'll stay here."

"Oh no," my father said. "Oh no, we've come this far . . ." He trailed off. There was too much to say. It seemed in our family there was always too much to say.

"Listen, Evy Jo," said Carol, "you've got to rouse yourself!"

There was a mirror in the room and I blew on the glass while Carol talked. I wrote "Corky" in the breath mist with a finger.

"You get up!" said Carol, suddenly passionate. "This is a big day! It's Steve and Corky's day! Fix your makeup and let's go!"

I wasn't sure what I was feeling as my sister spoke.

The poet Emily Dickinson once wrote to a friend asking if growth could be taught or, as she put it: "Is it unconveyed like melody or witchcraft?"

I'd been through a month of unprecedented growth. It wasn't melody or witchcraft. It had come from the lessons conveyed by Linda and Kylie and Corky.

I saw my mother's sadness and felt tenderness for

her. I wasn't practiced in this. It was enough, I thought, to feel a new appreciation for my life and the lives of others. Corky and Guiding Eyes had helped me become more expansive on the inside, where our undisclosed decencies draw breath.

* * *

Enter Bill and Reba Burkett, Corky's puppy raisers. Seeing them, Corky performed a move known at Guiding Eyes as "the Boomer Bounce." She jumped up and down, pushing her front paws off the floor while her hind feet remained planted. The bounce was a trait of her father, Boomer, a stud dog. All of Boomer's progeny had the bounce. The bounce often came first thing in the morning. I'd wake to find Corky going up and down clutching one of my running shoes in her mouth.

We were in a throng: graduates and their families and a host of puppy raisers, and it was a strange jamboree. But I had enough confidence in Corky to take her harness off and let her roam free with her first family. And Corky did exactly what I thought she'd do: she flopped on the ground, stuck her four feet in the air, put on a dog smile, and said, "Ah, rub my belly!" Bill and Reba rubbed her all over. They were delighted.

Corky and the Burketts had a backstory so intense I saw the only thing to do was hand them her leash. "Please take her for a walk," I said, "and take your time." There was something about Bill and Reba. They believed in dogs and people. They were radiant.

When they came back Corky had that smile you see on dogs who've achieved total happiness. Reba said something that knocked me off my pins: "You're exactly the right person for Miss Corky. I don't know why," she said, "but we always thought Corky should be with someone who loves books—maybe a student or professor."

"What a kind thing to say," I said, adding, "but Corky is the smart one in this unit."

Proving I was at least partially daft I demonstrated my "Swedish Chef" belly-rub technique— massaging Corky's chest while gibbering in fake Swedish like the famous character from Sesame Street.

Bill Burkett was a high school teacher—the one you always wanted but probably didn't have—smart, affirming, and steady. Reba was big-hearted and optimistic and in the course of conversation I learned that she and Bill and their kids, Ann and Bill Jr., had raised three other GEB dogs. Puppy raising was a family affair.

It was an affair filled with conversations, walks, play-time, dog obedience, trips in the car, high school foot-ball games with puppies in tow. I couldn't resist making a silent comparison with my own family. Next to the Burketts my mother and father were like hermits—in our house we each lived in a separate cave and seldom talked to one another. Somehow, among a dozen puppy-raising families and with Corky and the Burketts stand-ing beside me I thought of Karl Jaspers—the German psychoanalyst and philosopher who believed that de-cisions made today project backwards and change our past. It was a gentle thought. My blindness, my dog, my heart, would now become simple. Things had always been simple had I only known it.

Then we were all going home. The students left Guiding Eyes in a van with Linda at the wheel. We set out for LaGuardia airport some forty miles distant with our suitcases and laughter and dogs. Along with Corky and myself, there were three additional home-bound teams on the early morning airline run. "From now on," I thought, "it's all real . . ." Then I thought, "*Real*, what kind of word is that?" "Okay," I thought, "we're headed to the streets without training wheels—

man and dog—crisp and new, togetherness the premise of life."

"Here we come," I thought. "Here we come, man and dog taking on the commercial shabbiness of LaGuardia."

Aaron, Tina, and Sally were with me. Aaron was headed to Jackson, Mississippi. Sally was flying to Denver. Tina lived in Houston. I was the only freshman. The others had been flying with dogs for years.

"Listen," said Linda, "at LaGuardia all your flights are departing from the same terminal. Aaron, Tina, and Sally—you guys wait at McDonald's while I show Steve how to get through the metal detector."

"Oh you're in for some fun now!" said Sally, who'd said almost nothing during class.

"What do you mean?" I asked.

"You'll see," she said.

"It's always an encounter," said Aaron. "Sometimes the security officers know what they're doing, sometimes they don't."

"I've had security cops try to take my dog away from me," said Tina. "And they're not supposed to do that."

"What did you do?" I asked.

"I told him I'd trade my dog for his car."

"How'd that work out for you?" asked Linda.

"Sometimes they laugh, sometimes they don't," said Tina. "You should never let them take your dog for any reason," she added.

"That's right," said Linda. "Don't let anyone take your dog."

"So what's the big deal?" I asked.

"It's not a big deal," said Linda. "You have your dog sit and stay. Then you walk through the metal detector. Then you call her. She comes through. Because of the harness and collar she sets off the alarm. The guard must pat down your dog to make sure she's not a safety risk. All guide dogs are allowed on airplanes. No ifs, ands, or buts . . .

"Whatever you do, don't let someone walk away with your dog or remove her equipment," Linda added.

"Yeah," said Sally, "but some security people act like you're trying to walk through with an enormous fucking spider!"

"I'd pay to see that," said Aaron. "Or pay to have Linda describe it . . ."

"It's really not a big deal," said Linda. "Just be calm and cool."

* * *

Once we were all inside LaGuardia and my classmates were installed at McDonald's, and we'd said tearful and funny good-byes, Linda walked me to the security station.

"Okay," said Linda. "Have her sit."

Corky sat.

"Walk on through," said Linda.

I walked through the metal detector. No beep.

"Now call her," Linda said.

I called Corky. She scampered through the little archway and stopped beside me. The machine beeped.

"Does the dog bite?" asked the security man.

No one had prepared me for this question.

I was indignant on Corky's behalf like a mother whose child is accused of stealing candy.

"Of course she doesn't bite," I said. "She's a guide dog!"

"Everyone bites," said the security guard.

"Okay," I said. "But she's safe."

"I have to pat her down," he said.

"She'll really like that," I said.

He ran his hands over her back, touched the harness gingerly. Corky liked it. Wagged her tail.

"She's clean," he said.

I turned and waved to Linda. Our flight was boarding. We entered the Jetway.

Damn! I thought. *I'm getting on an airplane with a dog. And from now on I'll be going every place with her.* I supposed my composite feeling of wonder mixed with folly would be familiar to new parents leaving the hospital with their first child. Suddenly the world and everything in it was both vivid and strange.

Chapter Fifteen

Home. How to convey it? Corky entered and my apartment, with its high windows and long rooms, and the ambient space, was utterly different. It was simple—I was beaming and my dog was eager and I turned her loose so she could explore every inch of her home and this she obediently did in the manner of all dogs by alertly sniffing every corner, walking from room to room. Her happiness swelled in the air. I sat on the sofa where the former me had been so damned sad. It struck me it was just six months since I'd faced the plastic-lemon man and been told that life ahead would be next to impossible. On the day of the lemon man I'd walked Ithaca's streets and nearly been killed. Now we were home, man and canine companion. That things were better was true, entirely true. Corky returned to me with a running shoe in her mouth.

Our life together began. I thought we should go outside and wander around.

"We will go walking with no purpose," I thought.

"This is the first day of our team. It's the first time we'll travel without a guide-dog trainer."

I had no idea where to go. Ambling seemed the best plan.

"Let the world sort things out," I thought.

Straightaway we went downtown. It was a bright day and a new life so I thought I should go someplace I'd never been. On the first block I decided to enter a hat shop; a boutique; a store filled with crescent hats on mannequin heads. To me they were splotches of color; weird as a Kandinsky painting, lovely. And there I was, a man in a hat shop with a dog. I felt giddy, fantastically alive. "Life is better with a Labrador," I thought. "Blindness is behind me," I thought—that is, I'd imagined I would never feel inferior again. But the next few minutes would unfold like a painted Chinese fan with a tightly scripted story about culture and disability. I was too happy to guess Corky and her poet were about to be a complication.

The shopkeeper wanted to know what I was doing there. She landed directly in front of me like a jumping spider.

I saw a burgundy thing, a wide-brimmed felt fedora the color of cranberries. I caressed it. Corky sat and admired me touching the thing. It was a moment of small, contained aesthetic pleasure.

"What are you doing?" asked the shopkeeper. Her tone of voice was reproving. It was a tone that said, "Why on earth are you here?" She'd fumbled her opening gambit—hadn't said "Can I help you?" or "What are you looking for?" (I imagined she didn't know if blind people "look" for anything . . . Was it okay to say "look?"—maybe it wasn't—so she said "What are you doing?")

"A fedora," I said. "A mauve fedora!"

"Well, yes," said the shopkeeper, who was backing away from us.

(She wanted to know how I "knew" it was a rose-purple fedora but couldn't ask. She imagined all blind people see nothing. This is a common presumption.)

"A mauve fedora," I said again because I liked saying it.

"Mmmm," said the shopkeeper. Then she said, "Maybe you can take the dog outside?"

"No," I said. "The dog stays. It's the law.

"*Indifférence violet*," I said then with a bad French accent.

The shopkeeper stared.

"*Je veux acheter un chapeau pour mon chien,*" I said.

"You want to buy a hat for your dog?" she asked.

"Yes," I said. "I want to buy her the mauve fedora."

"Oh dear!" she said.

"I might decide to buy two," I said.

"One for my sister, one for my dog," I said.

In the end I didn't buy any hats . . . but I walked away knowing for the first time that the freedom to go places with a guide dog didn't mean I'd be treated warmly. I'd have to do the work of being pleased with myself—which meant being pleased with ourselves . . . We were just a man and dog prowling for fashion.

"We can be misunderstood and stylish," I thought.

* * *

It was a warm day. We walked around Ithaca's tiny downtown. I'd gone into a hat shop first thing because the freedom of having a service dog meant spontaneity. Every little place could be Paris—Joni Mitchell's Paris, where one is "unfettered and alive." That's how I felt about it. And though I thought I knew the Morris Frank story—knew there might still be occasional moments of opposition to a guide dog in public—I didn't foresee the awkwardness and uncomprehending silence that greeted us in a millinery store.

We walked an ordinary street . . . houses, shops, a few churches . . . and Corky was so fully confident.

"This must be what sighted people feel like," I thought as we climbed a steep hill. "You're just you." The idea was both banal and oddly original. "You're just you, or we're just us," I said aloud.

We approached Cornell University. Corky stopped in her tracks—looked left and right and didn't budge. "What the hell is it?" I thought. "A hole in the pavement?" But no, it was a Volkswagen, abandoned, awaiting the cops, evidence of some student misadventure.

Why hadn't Corky stepped off the sidewalk and gone around it? She was trained to look for detours. Instead she'd backed up, dragging me along. Then a policeman appeared.

"That's one smart dog," he said.

"Just off the sidewalk there's a hole about five feet deep."

I remembered what they said back at Guiding Eyes about praising your dog and I "loved her up."

"Hey," said the policeman, "I've always wondered, do guide dogs know their owners are blind?"

"No," I said, "they think we're clueless!" We shared a laugh. But there was truth behind the joke. A guide dog knows her human needs assistance—not sometimes but always. She knows her job is to keep on task wherever we go.

After the tow truck hauled the car away I invited the policeman to have a cup of coffee in a nearby bagel place. Much to my surprise he accepted. We talked about dogs. "Have you ever heard of Sergeant Stubby?" he asked.

"Yes," I said, "wasn't he a military dog in World War I?"

"Yeah, he served with the troops in the trenches."

"His story is wild," he said, adding, "By the way, I'm Joe."

After introducing myself and Miss Corky I said, "If I remember correctly, Stubby turned up on the Yale University football field while the troops were drilling."

"Yes, and a soldier named Robert Conroy took a shining to him and smuggled him aboard the troop ship," said Joe. "He fought with the 102nd Infantry in France—he learned how to warn the troops of gas attacks; he located the wounded; he even bit a German spy on the ass."

"There's another great thing about Stubby," I said.

"When Conroy went to law school at Georgetown after the war, Stubby went with him. He's the mascot of the Hoyas."

"He fought in seventeen battles," said Joe. "Can you imagine?"

* * *

I was having conversations with strangers. In a diner, the owner, an old Greek man, wanted to give Corky some sausage links. I explained she couldn't have any human food. "That's crazy!" he said, and he pushed three sausages into my hand. I stuffed them in the pocket of my coat. "Thank you," I said. "I'll give them to her later."

"That dog's a hero!" he said. "You have to feed heroes!"

"Oh I know," I said.

"My uncle was blind," said the proprietor as he wiped the counter.

"He lived to be a hundred," he said.

This was the life I'd always wanted: being out and about, engaging in casual talk. Though I was uncomfortable with the heroism shtick, I was talking to someone I scarcely knew and he was admitting us into his tribe.

* * *

A couple of weeks later the Ithaca newspaper ran a story about Corky. It was a good piece about a poet and his dog. I said something about poems and walking. There were some nice photographs. It was a small and positive accomplishment. Then the phone rang.

The voice was pure gravel.

"I don't know you," she said, "but I've read about you."

"Oh yes," I said.

"Well," she said, "I'm the president of the local garden club. We're a group of women who talk about nature. We thought it would be wonderful if you would come to our next meeting. You know, just talk about guide dogs."

I pictured a tasteful sunroom, a dozen women, and a tea trolley.

What harm could there be in it? "Why not be an ambassador for the guide-dog school?" I thought.

The woman, whose name was Sarah Bookmier, sent a limo to get us. I should have been somewhat suspicious of a garden party at night but I wasn't. I'd never been to such a thing before. Corky and I climbed into a Lincoln with a largely silent uniformed driver. I didn't know where we were going and for some reason it never occurred to me to ask. I was attending a party at a farm. I had my dog.

How bad could it be? The car eventually came to a stop and the door swung open and there was Mrs. Bookmier.

I found it wasn't a garden party at all, but an Amway meeting—the event was about recruiting women to sell cleaning products. A dozen of us were treated to a film about soap and stain removers. We sat uneasily on hard chairs while rain beat at the windows. I did my best to smile.

I stroked Corky's ears—the dog as familiar, my Labrador as lucky blanket. I was in the country home of Mrs. Bookmier-Sparkle. We were captive in her temple. We'd sell soap and she'd become the queen of soap and our chairs squeaked and every now and then wind punched the roof.

When the film was over and it was time for discussion, Mrs. Bookmier made a pitch about financial independence through soap, which meant selling lots of soap, and in turn, recruiting more people to sell soap.

Mrs. Bookmier looked my way. She said blind people were poor—weren't they? And why couldn't I recruit an army of blind soap sellers and make sightless people rich? I could, couldn't I?

One woman named Bethany spoke up and said:

"How can Stephen know every blind person? Do you think blind people just hang out together?"

I loved her for saying it. But Mrs. Bookmier sailed on:

"He can call all the guide-dog users, they must have a network," she said.

I said something about privacy laws.

Then it got worse. Mrs. Bookmier said the problem with disabled people was that they didn't have a work ethic.

I decided to escape. I had no idea if the Lincoln was outside. I reckoned with Corky by my side I could hitchhike back to Ithaca. The unknown didn't bother me. It was a new feeling. I'd barely been home a month from Guiding Eyes and I felt wholly independent.

I walked downhill in the rain with Corky jingling beside me. When we reached the bottom of Bookmier's twisted drive the Lincoln pulled up. "They didn't tell us about moments like this in guide-dog school," I said to Corky, who shook her dog tags in reply.

*   *   *

Civic life with a disability is theatrical. I hadn't fully known this. I'd been so busy trying to play the role of a dashing nondisabled lad, the impossibly healthy boy of American imagination, that I'd failed to appreciate what being myself would be like. Corky had brought me into the land of Prospero, where the world was a stage, where each location was nuanced and required negotiation in ways I'd not imagined. Sometimes we were accepted and sometimes not. I found my reception could change in an instant. I could be admired as a blind traveler and in the same hour face opposition. I discovered this upside-downside drama was consistent, and whether I liked it or not, I now had to perform with mixed emotions on a very real stage.

I wrote in my journal:

I'm right here and I'm immensely inconvenient. A blind man at a garden party. Blind man in a comic book store. Built environs are designed to keep our kind out. Our kind includes those who direct their wheelchairs by breathing, amble with their crutches, speak with signs, type to talk, roll oxygen tanks, or ask for large-print menus. We are here. And our placement is insufficiently understood in public. Which came first, these blues or the architecture that keeps us always inconvenient?

To perform disability meant affirming its place in the village square. Whenever possible it also meant the cultivation of irony.

I walked downtown to get a haircut. Corky and I descended steps—the shop was below street level. A bell on the door chimed as we entered. Men were talking as we came in but they turned silent when they saw us. I wondered if there was a word for a group of men gone quiet. No one bothered to speak. The sight of a man and dog had violated house custom. I shut the door carefully. The bell wasn't cheerful. "Christ," I thought, "even the bell is against us." Still no one said a thing. I thought: "Disability scares some folks. They have no words for it. On a primitive level they may believe disability is contagious like influenza, or worse, it's the evil eye."

I had to be the one to break the ice. I went for a dog joke. "Hey, my dog needs a trim," I said. That was all it took for the boys to snap back to life. It was like I'd said "abracadabra." There was old-guy laughter. "Great," said the barber, "take a seat." I took a seat. Corky lay down.

But then they went quiet again. I realized the men weren't getting trims or shaves. The barber's place was their social club and my arrival had dampened things. Even the radio wasn't helping, as it was tuned to static. Corky rattled her chain. The scene was exceedingly strange. Rather than tossing out another joke I kept silent, wanting to see what would happen. I thought the barber might throw out a cliché—something like: "We don't get many dogs in here," to which I'd reply, "No wonder, at prices like these." But it wasn't the barber who broke the silence. One of the men said: "My friend, who I served with in Korea, he went blind—he got a seeing-eye dog back around 'fifty-five." Then I understood their silence. It wasn't the oddness of a blind man and his dog, or disability superstition that had kept them quiet. It was memory.

*   *   *

Up and down the streets we went. It was half sunny and then it would threaten to snow. April. Upstate New York.

In a moment trees would be turning green. With my meager sight I'd see the new leaves as yellow smoke. It would be our first changing season together. I recited "Sumer is icumen in . . . and the forest sings anew . . ." Then I sang it. I couldn't tell whether Corky liked my singing or not. As a matter of human vanity I decided she did. Or I told myself she didn't mind. It was a turning season of newfound pleasure.

That's when I decided I'd go to New York. To be sure, there'd be plenty of good and bad experiences in

Manhattan. But what mattered was the spontaneity of walking. It felt as though Corky and I had conquered Ithaca in two weeks and I'd always wanted to go to New York solo. Now I could do something nearly as good. I could go with a Labrador.

Chapter Sixteen

The doorman at the Algonquin Hotel on Forty-Fourth Street loved the sight of us as we uncoiled from a taxi, Corky's tail wagging, ears up, appearing to smile. And the doorman seemed equally pleased. "Now that's a great dog!" he said, "she's a champ!" We stood together on the sidewalk and by God if everyone didn't seem happy. A couple of tourists asked if they could take our picture. "Of course," I said. "Of course." This was our first hotel as a guide-dog team. It was going nicely. The doorman was named Charlie. He wore a top hat and a black coat with gold braid. He appeared pleased both with his job and our sudden appearance. Upside: welcoming man. At the front desk Charlie introduced us as Stephen and Corky the Champ.

He insisted on giving us a private tour of the hotel. We saw the Rose Room and the famous Round Table where in the 1920s writers Dorothy Parker, Robert Benchley, George S. Kaufman and others gathered daily for lunch and savage gossip. In the dark Edwardian lobby Charlie introduced Corky to Mary Bodne, widow of the hotel's former owner Ben Bodne. Mary in turn introduced us to Matilda, the hotel cat.

* * *

Charlie was so happy I thought he might stay with us all afternoon. I'd reserved the room formerly occupied by James Thurber and Charlie lingered, describing all the pictures on the walls.

* * *

We were in a good dream all day: Corky and I walked the Brooklyn Bridge. The sky was blue-going-to-green as we raced along the promenade deck. It was easy to imagine men in swallow-tailed coats and women with wide hats approaching. Blindness was all mist for me and yet the dear light was wonderful. For people like me light is a mystery—a literal one, less of physics, more a matter of interpretation. I live in unfocused brilliance. We were going very fast in a jogger's reverie, Corky and I. We passed two slow runners. I wondered what Corky's waking dream was like.

I thought how a dog's vision must be like widescreen cinema—what they used to call Panavision—the whole world must be wide and bright for a dog. The entire day must be like watching *Ben-Hur*—a sequence of dazzling chariot races. It was amusing to think of it. Every day is a big-screen Hollywood spectacle for a dog.

* * *

In Macy's I made the mistake of talking to a mannequin. Every blind person has done this. A woman said, "That man won't be talkin'," and laughed and walked with me to the men's department. Bonding meant I couldn't be embarrassed—it felt as if some essential part of my self-regard had been fired in a kiln. "Thank you Corky," I said. "Thank you, girl!"

I was a little bit like Charlie Chaplin—easy, loose jointed, mistake prone and strong.

* * *

Small things: she walked me around a sidewalk elevator, its doors revealing steep stairs. New York: the city of ominous basements.

She stopped at a curb, then backed up. A double-decker tourist bus was drifting, scraping street signs, the people up top laughing—the bus was like a boat filled with drunks. Good girl.

We walked past odd little shops, their doors open, releasing Victorian odors of commerce—New York is a city of smells—many unidentifiable—the scent of earth from one door; fragrance of plums from another. On Sixth Avenue a woman ran out of a shop and grabbed my arm. "You must taste," she said. "Taste?" I said. "Yeah, you taste!" She dragged us into a Chinese bakery and offered us a Chinese cocktail bun, filled with coconut. Corky and I rewarded her with a little dance. New York. Everyone feels vaguely as if he or she is in a circus. What can you do? You chew, dance, and walk. You thank strangers who suddenly appear. Do they appreciate your soul? Do they have pity for you? You don't know.

I felt there had to be a better word than *bonding*. I was living the chaos of joy, something one can't talk about with ease, largely because there's no vocabulary for the thing—you're in love with your surroundings, loving a barefoot mind, wild to go anyplace. Sometimes crossing Fifth Avenue felt like traveling to the top of Mount Olympus. The hot dog vendor on the corner was Zeus. I could tell.

We bought a bag of wild cherries from a fruit stand. Stood beside a fountain. Touched the hair on skinny trees.

* * *

George Eliot wrote:

"We long for an affection altogether ignorant of our faults. Heaven has accorded this to us in the uncritical canine attachment."

By day two in Manhattan I saw George Eliot was incorrect. Corky wasn't ignorant of my faults at all. Working through the tangled places she surmised my confusions. Stopping before a flight of subway steps she looked up at my face, wanting to be certain I'd found my location and that my footing was secure.

And the caresses of the subway dark! A softness like twilight under the city! The anteroom of hell with its stink of burnt rubber and urine and the collected odor of ten million human fears—and we were forging ahead through the damasked air and I don't know how to convey it—but the rhythms of the trains and our own courage were tightly bound. Who the hell is happy in the subway? I swear we were.

* * *

Our session in New York underscored both our safety and happiness. Now and then we had to stop someplace just so I could hug her—we found a bench outside of FAO Schwarz, the famous toy store, and I took her harness off and scratched her chest. And then she flopped over, demanding a belly rub. And wouldn't you know it? Two children from Germany, a boy and girl, about ten years old, accompanied by their mother—they wanted to help give Corky a belly rub . . . we had a spontaneous belly-rub klatsch. Then more people came. A dozen. People unbeknownst to each other, drawn by softness and animal faith in the heart of a great city. "Animal faith" was philosopher George Santayana's term for instinctive belief, belief without rational foundation. I'd begun using the term for my own purposes—walking with Cork was opening the hours for me. I was feeling a foundational confidence and openness I'd never known. Perhaps this wasn't rational. But maybe it was? Animals keep us alive to perceptions we've long given up on. I'd always kind of imagined this was true. Now I was experiencing it. Our belly-rub klatsch was a little impromptu church ceremony. Afternoon sunlight was reflected by tall windows. Children and adults were laughing. Corky had all four feet in the air and a wizened dog smile.

Our last "trial" day in the city had to involve a long

walk in Central Park. We entered somewhere around Seventy-Second Street at Fifth Avenue and made our way to the boat pond. I walked with my eyes closed. I'd always suffered from tremendous eye pain and Corky's skill allowed me to rest them, to give up on the desperation of residual sight. It was a late April day and the scent of new grass was on the wind. And from a distance we heard boaters laughing on the water.

Someone had a portable radio playing Beethoven's Fifth Symphony. I felt a lovely, tempered joy among trees.

I remembered Joseph Campbell once saying: "You must have a room or a certain hour of the day or so, where you do not know who your friends are, you don't know what you owe anybody or what they owe you—but a place where you can simply experience and bring forth what you are and what you might be . . ."

For us, that place was now anywhere . . .

Chapter Seventeen

Corky was changing me into someone who could think more clearly. Being more engaged in public helped me see some of my mental mistakes. For instance, if I wasn't alone anymore, what was sadness but a posture?

The silver birches outside my apartment in Ithaca were brilliant. The day was as glossy and brilliant as an old Kodachrome. Corky sat at a tall window while I wrote. She kept her privacies and watched the world go by. Because of her stoic happiness I started asking questions. What exactly did Corky radiate? She loved me; saved me from cars; but she also rested entirely in affirming, companionable silences. She was the first creature to teach me such a thing. Better I thought than a shelf full of poetry. Better than my family.

When I was very small I didn't know I'd meet people who wouldn't like me until one afternoon, climbing stairs with my father, my hand in his, we met an elderly Swedish woman who lived just below us and who said "Tsk, tsk" because I was blind. I was only four and it was winter in Helsinki. This had been a foundational moment for me as such moments are for all sensitive children—it's the very second we sense we're not who we've met in the mirror, or having no mirror, we're not who our parents say we are. Cruelty is one way we arrive. It comes without warning like branches tapping a window. "She's a fool," my father said, as if that solved the riddle of human embarrassment.

Maybe it wasn't ridiculous at all to imagine a more optimistic life. I began thinking such things. "I'll be damned," I thought. "With Corky I could now feel sorry for the gray Swedish matron."

I saw she was a picture of absolute loneliness. I was patting Corky on the head. Who hurt the old Swedish woman who lived downstairs? Was it her White Russian husband who beat her and her children and then died at fifty having drunk away her dowry?

* * *

Discovering that with a dog I was a figure of more than passing interest called for gumption and patience but I was getting it. In a convenience store, late at night, where Corky and I had stopped for a bottle of milk, a man pushing a mop shouted: "Hey, there's a service dog!" Then another man suddenly appeared from the back and asked if I knew the story of the Prophet Muhammad and the hero dog. "No," I said. "Well the dog Kitmir is in paradise!" he said. "He was a hero like your dog!" "Hero dog! Hero dog!" said the first man, waving the mop. I had no name for my emotion. It was a weird transport, half affirming, half embarrassing. What was I to make of this? In one store I might be a problem, in another a mythology.

The two of us were unconditionally stirring to strangers. Sometimes we were approached by doe-eyed holy-roller types—people who'd grown up watching Jerry Lewis telethons, who'd absorbed a thousand sermons about the blind, who need the grace of God—wanting to touch us, pray for us, or at the very least, tell us how uplifting we were. Riding a bus from Ithaca to Geneva, and feeling good, Corky tucked under the seat, a woman seated across from us said: "You and your dog just gave me some Jesus!" I was crippled Tim, a vision of Christ's mercy.

These benedictions occurred so often I started worrying about it. When would it occur? On a bus in Ithaca a woman said loudly: "Can I pray for you?" I couldn't help myself and replied: "Yes, madam, you may pray for me, but only if together, you and I, raise our prayers for all the good people on this bus who have trouble brewing inside, their cancers aborning even as we speak, whose children have gone astray through substance abuse, people who even now feel lost in a sea of troubles, let us pray, all together, for our universal salvation." I clutched her arm with feverish intensity. The bus pulled to a routine stop and she jumped out the door. Passengers applauded. "Don't take it personally," a woman said to me then. I smiled. But how else to take it?

I asked Edward, an Episcopal priest whom I met in a coffee shop, what he thought of the "public Jesus complex," as I'd come to call it. We sat on a park bench drinking coffee out of paper cups, Corky chewing on a bone at our feet.

"Many Christians don't like the body," he said. "That's how they understand the Crucifixion. They think the body is the throwaway part of Christ. And of course that's entirely wrong: the body of Jesus is, as Dietrich Bonhoeffer said: the living temple of God and of the new humanity.

"In effect," he said, "every body is the body of Jesus. Which means each body, broken or not, is a true body, imbued with spirit, and not a sign of want. There's a beauty to the diversity in the body of Christ."

"So why do I meet so many predatory prayer slingers who want to mumble over me?" I asked.

"The insecure ye will always have with ye . . ." Edward said.

* * *

With a service dog you become a "sacred/profane wandering totem" and there's no help for it. After half a year with Corky I started seeing this as hopscotch: jump—you're in a beautiful, even magical space; jump—you're in a profane spot. Jump again—you're like the dog Kitmir in paradise. Jump. You're fighting with a connoisseur of hate who you'll find almost anywhere and without warning.

"What if a warm reception is always conditional?" I asked Corky.

She answered by looking up me. She demanded I be honest. Our acceptance rate was nearly 90 percent.

If I wanted to feel persecuted I'd have to recognize the impulse and weigh it. Eleanor Roosevelt once said no one can make you feel bad about yourself without your permission. Something to that effect.

Still you have to be tough. It's a jungle out there.

I was guarded when a woman wearing what I thought was a raccoon coat approached us in the cereal aisle of a Manhattan supermarket and said: "Oh I just love guide dogs!"

"Me too," I said.

"I mean," she said, "I really love them!"

"Remember you're not in a terrible hurry," I thought. I reminded myself that chance conversations inevitably reflect shy fascinations—this is where culture comes from.

Beside a mountain of corn flakes she told me about her cousin who raised guide-dog puppies. She said her husband had a blind roommate in college who'd had a dog. She described her own dog, a German shorthaired pointer.

Dogs make blindness approachable. "Approachable" blindness means "easy to talk to" blindness.

But the motives of strangers have many origins.

In LaGuardia Airport, waiting for a flight, an elderly woman turned up suddenly and said: "I had a dog like that once."

"Oh yes," I said.

"Yeah, someone poisoned it," she said.

"Oh dear," I said.

She regarded us for a few seconds and then turned away.

In a diner on lower Broadway, a man, disheveled and clattering, someone the locals seemed to know, wandered from table to table interrupting breakfasters, pressing into each person's space, piercing the brains of strangers. He called a cop "Porky" and an elderly woman "Grandma" as he lurched steadily toward me. "Oh doggy!" he said. "Doggy doggy doggy!"

Then he said, "What kind of fucking person are you?"

I tried my best Robert De Niro impression: "Are you talking to ME?"

He wasn't amused.

"A prisoner!" he shouted, for the whole diner was his stage. "This dog's a prisoner!"

For a moment I felt the rising heat of embarrassment and rejection. Then, as he repeated my dog was a slave, I softened. In a moment of probable combat I stepped far back inside myself, not because I had to, but how to say it? Corky was unruffled. She actually nuzzled my leg. The nuzzle went up my torso, passed through my neck, went straight for the amygdala.

I smiled then. I said, "You're right. And I'm a prisoner too."

I don't know if it was my smile or my agreement that did the trick, but he backed up, turned, and walked out the door. Strangers applauded.

I'd beaten a lifetime of bad habits. I hadn't fallen into panic, or rage, or felt a demand to flee.

I sat at the counter, tucked Corky safely out of the way of walking customers, and ordered some eggs. I daydreamed over coffee.

When I was eleven years old I fell onto a pricker bush. It's hard to say how I did it, but I was impaled by hundreds of thorns. My sister, who was six at the time, and my cousin Jim, who was maybe nine, fell to the ground laughing as if they might die. I begged them for help, which of course only made them laugh all the harder. I remember tears welling in my eyes and their insensible joy. I also knew in that moment they were right to laugh—that I was the older kid, was a bit bossy, disability be damned. I was the one who told my sister and cousin what to do. Now I was getting mine. My just deserts. In the end I tore myself from the monster shrub and stormed into the house. I sulked while they continued laughing outside.

Perhaps I thought, there in the diner, I could live in a new and more flexible way.

"Is it as simple as this?" I thought. "One simply decides to breathe differently."

I saw, in a way, it was that simple.

Saw also how a dog can be your teacher. And while eating wheat toast I thought of the Buddha's words from the Dhammapada:

> *Live in Joy, In love,*
> *Even among those who hate.*
> *Live in joy, In health,*
> *Even among the afflicted.*
> *Live in joy, In peace,*
> *Even among the troubled.*
> *Look within. Be still.*
> *Free from fear and attachment,*
> *Know the sweet joy of living in the way.*

Chapter Eighteen

I needed to find a job. I wanted an engaged life. Notice: blind poet seeks employment. I licked envelopes and stuffed them in the mail. Was it my imagination or did rejections come as fast as I posted the letters? Certainly the odds were steep. I applied for government assistance: section 8 housing, food stamps, social security disability. I took a steep financial penalty and cashed in my modest retirement savings from a decade of adjunct teaching. I applied to arts colonies where writers and artists are housed while they work. I wore a path in the pavement between my apartment and the Ithaca post office. The postmaster loved seeing Corky and gave her biscuits. She started turning automatically toward the federal building whether we were headed there or not.

Yes, when we're in love we admire everything. I was more optimistic than I'd ever been. I suspected this made very little difference where fate was concerned. But persistence changes us. Acceptances arrived. Though I didn't get any job interviews I was admitted to three arts retreats. It was now time to leave home. What's the premise of living? That life wants us? Silly. Maybe. But I packed two oversize duffel bags—one for me, one for Cork.

Our first stop was the MacDowell Colony in Peterborough, New Hampshire. Though MacDowell was founded in 1907 and had been supporting artists for nearly a century, I learned Corky would be their first guide dog. We'd be pioneers. We'd be like Morris Frank among the artists. I thought, quite self-consciously, we'd have to be exceptional guests. Meanwhile I imagined us walking in the woods where Aaron Copland, Leonard Bernstein, and James Baldwin had wandered. "It's a place for ambling," I told Corky.

* * *

The MacDowell Colony was the perfect place for a new guide-dog team. The colony gives fortunate artists individual studios in the woods where they're free to work in solitude. Twice daily people gather for breakfast and dinner in Colony Hall, a building that was once a hay barn. The rest of the time you're on your own. There are almost no cars. You can walk in the woods and think. The place offers creative people a paradise.

Our visit to MacDowell signaled the start of my blended life with Corky—that is, it provided a first glimpse of how we'd be perceived in group space. Mingling with artists I found I was quite often in disability-centric situations, even over something as simple as a meal. This had nothing to do with MacDowell. The staff couldn't have been kinder or more receptive. But I learned quickly that artists, many of them academics, had very little understanding of physical difference.

As we were queuing up for dinner a woman shouted: "Oh my God, a DOG! A DOG! A DOG!"

"This is Corky," I said.

"Are you blind?" the woman asked.

"Yes, Corky is an actual guide dog," I said.

"You wanna touch my face?" the woman asked.

"I'm too inhibited for that," I said.

"Can I touch your face?" she asked.

"I might be too inhibited for that too," I said.

"C'mon, touch my face," she said.

I was saved by a staff member who guided us to a table with three classical composers.

"I think he's blind," said a woman. She said it under her breath. Presumably for the edification of the man immediately to her left.

"Evidently," said the man. "That's a guide dog."

"The man is blind but he can hear rather well," I said.

"Oh yes, that's right!" said the man who introduced himself as Charles.

The whisper woman said her name was Wendy.

"I'm Dolores," said a second woman.

Each was a musician and composer.

"This is Corky," I said, "she's a multimedia artist." This got a laugh. "She's from New York," I said. "She has a tattoo and dresses in leather."

"Can we pet her?" asked Dolores.

"The thing is, she's not a house pet," I said.

"When she's wearing her harness she doesn't want you to address her. She's trained to ignore people while wearing her gear—even when lying quietly under a table."

"But she's not working now," said Dolores.

"Yes, she is," I said. "Staying quiet is work."

"But it can't ruin her to just have a little petting?" said Dolores.

"Well yes it can," I said. "She has to go to restaurants and be completely inconspicuous. This is her professionalism. All service dogs must have this capacity to focus—that's why guide dogs won the right to travel in public."

And so it began—explaining things. Dolores sniffed that casual petting couldn't possibly ruin my dog. It was the start of a routine, outlining the dos and don'ts of interacting with service dogs. In the years to come I'd meet many people like Dolores, dog lovers who believe their special connection with animals means the rules don't apply to them. I even discovered a word for this—*biophilia*. The term was coined by Edward O. Wilson, the famed Harvard entomologist who wrote: "Humanity is exalted not because we are so far above other living creatures, but because knowing them well elevates the very concept of life." This is true and one may think of this as ecopsychology. We're healthiest when we're in deep and productive relations with all beings. But what I found was how few people understand working dogs in general and blindness in particular. The concept that a dog might enjoy her work was foreign to many. Some pet owners are quite opinionated. Guiding Eyes hadn't prepared me for interactions with this kind of vanity—what I'd eventually call *auto-biophilia*—a Romantic belief that because you think you're special you have a unique bond with animals. Guide-dog users often meet people who are spiritually unfulfilled and who overcompensate with dogs. They're the Doctor Dolittles; the PETA propagandists; the New Age types. They're put out when you insist on following working-dog etiquette. Some even try to slip your dog dinner rolls under the table.

Just as Corky was the subject of conversation, so was blindness. I didn't want to talk about blindness. I'd have preferred discussing Henry James.

Instead we talked about being blind. I understood why. I discovered at Guiding Eyes that there aren't many blind people in the United States. The blind are always outliers, and strangers are curious. They ask: *Can you see anything? What can you see? Can you tell how many fingers I'm holding up? How can you write? How can you describe the world? Do you have dreams?*

I was in the dining room at a prestigious arts retreat, in a room where Yoko Ono once ate spaghetti and instead of discussing the arts I was describing light—that the blind can often see it, that many see colors. And that those who don't see anything at all still understand the world richly.

* * *

After dinner Corky and I walked on dirt roads under the stars. Fireflies sparkled in the hedges. We were not quite in heaven and not precisely on earth. When our path turned into the woods Corky guided me without a hitch—pulling me forward in the spicy air, the two of us liberated from dinnertime sociology.

In the dark I found I was in an expansive state of mind. We walked a long time in the night. I wondered how many things at once she could smell. The moon was out and the wood anemones, the white buttercups of New England, were shining like little moons. I knew this because I got down on my hands and knees and peered closely. "She must smell them," I thought. What about the bottle gentians in the wet thickets? Tiny blue flowers. What might they smell like? Every dog has three hundred million olfactory receptors in its nose. By contrast humans have only six million. A dog's brain has forty times our capacity for analyzing scents. Corky knew what was on the wind. Her world was entirely distinct from mine. We sat a long time in the woods and I let her scent deeply.

Our pauses, whether alone in the woods or on a street, occurred because we were safe. If contentment meant one thing it was this: our mutual security meant I could live in full measure.

* * *

In the mornings I wrote in my cabin. We had a nice rhythm. Corky lay on the daybed beside the desk while I worked on fragments of poems. Sometimes I'd stop and pace. I wondered self-consciously, elaborately, about the symbolism of blindness—not for the first time, but in a closed community like MacDowell I suspected some of the other artists perceived me in emblematic terms. I was a little sensitive, maybe paranoid. Did they see me as someone who's only effectual because of his dog? A student at Guiding Eyes told me many sighted people believe the blind are merely being pulled along by their dogs—that we're simply attached and follow in lockstep obedience. Did the others at MacDowell see us as competent? Should it matter? I picked up a vague discomfort evinced by some of the residents. When I joined a table of artists at dinner, sometimes conversation stopped. The man with the dog was there. One could fairly imagine them saying, "He isn't one of us." No one said it. But I'd have to restart the dinner talk. "Who wrote the most notes today?" I'd say if I was among composers. Mostly the talk turned to Corky. "What does she do for you exactly?" "How many commands does she know?" "How does she know when to cross the street?" "How does she find places for you?"

Of course I wanted to say: "How does Mozart help you?" "Is music finally anything more than cultivated time?"

But I answered their questions.

"No!" said a woman who wrote librettos, "the dog waits for you to decide when to cross the street?!"

She couldn't believe it. She seemed put out. A myth had been ruined for her. My guide dog was supposed to be smarter than me.

"It's actually a kind of deep faith," I said. "A dog won't do anything dangerous or take action that defies its best instinct."

"So?" she said. The information was somehow disappointing to her.

"It's simple, really," I said. "Corky won't step into harm's way. And she doesn't know where we're going. That's my job. Which means I have to study always—ask questions—know where I am. Moreover, my job is to trust people. Talk with strangers. If you like, my job is to dare to be in the world."

I went on: "And over time your dog loves you and you love her. Then something very interesting happens. 'You realize that behind the love is a person who hasn't given up. Who still walks about in his nail-studded boots and laughs because of love.' You understand your dog loves that person."

"That's a Labrador," I thought, "trained to guide me in traffic she admires a man who is both improbable and true." This I did not say. One should never reveal all his secrets.

* * *

It wasn't easy, this able-bodied people's disability complex. "Complex" was Carl Jung's term, and in psychoanalysis it means a core pattern of emotions, memories, and perceptions which are hidden from the conscious mind—buried traumas and the like. Disability bothered people or some of them. It was understandable. Disabled characters in drama and literature are invidious and often spell trouble. Maybe the disabled are vaguely dishonest. A woman who lived on the grounds of the MacDowell Colony—who wasn't an artist per se but had a house that was grandfathered in to the larger property—told employees I was faking my blindness because she saw me walking with Corky on a leash in the woods. That a guide dog sometimes gets "leash time" hadn't occurred to her. In her view I was cheating the system, bringing a pet into her domain.

It was genuinely hard thinking about that woman. Contemplating her pettiness was like having a tooth-ache in the soul. I was in the world but ineluctably separate, and if I was going to live without rancor or self-pity I'd have to become more philosophical. One afternoon I wrote a poem for Corky:

Running to the Wood

My dog, trained for the blind,
Sees Rorschachs of wings.
Vows of light, tongueless stones
Call her to the door.
All gods are avatars of width.
They dance a bone dance
Down the centuries of June.
Dispensed by mists, I'm lonely too.
The Roman gravity of our lives is inconsolable.

* * *

I thought of the gray flocks of people who don't understand disabilities, all those citizens with their own
wounds. "The last line of my poem was probably wrong,"
I thought. Our lives, my dog's and mine, were not fated
to suffer dark, supernatural storms like the characters in
Shakespeare's *Julius Caesar*. Just get out of the cabin and
take a walk, I told myself. And we did.

* * *

We decided to go into the nearby town. Peterborough
was one mile distant and the route required us to travel
on roads without sidewalks. Corky had been trained in
"shore lining," a technique to keep us on the shoulder
of the road. We were moving at a fast clip when she
pulled me into a ditch as a car raced past, just miss-
ing us. The driver didn't stop. I sat in the pine needles
and weeds and cried. The tears came in racking spasms.
They'd been long suppressed. I was crying in response
to Corky's great, life-saving maneuver and also because
life was precious and so very fragile. Corky licked my
tears and after a time we walked the rest of the way into
town.

We walked up and down the streets of Peterborough. "I am not who I used to be," I thought as we passed the old Congregationalist church. "I'm Corky's accomplishment. So that is really something."

I was talking to myself. Outside a hardware store a woman said, "Are you all right?"

I said I was all right.

* * *

Back in our cabin I translated a poem from Finnish, which contained the lines: "sometimes I see a child / see in him what I was like / and I want to say I'm sorry."

Corky lay beside the open door scenting the breeze. We sat side by side in the growing dusk. Wind stirred the maples.

Our companionship was intimate and richer than poems.

With every walk she found dancing leaves or raindrops, lizards, flowers. And me? I profited, standing in the grass, knowing of my smallness in the scheme of things—and it all felt good.

Chapter Nineteen

Though I still didn't have a job I had a vigorous life. Back in Ithaca I took Corky to the lake for a swim.

I thought I might work harder at becoming good-natured.

"Be kind," said Plato, "for everyone you meet is fighting a harder battle."

On the Ithaca Commons a very old man reached out to pat Corky. My first instinct was to reprimand him, but then I saw he was seriously ill. He said something I didn't understand. He was momentarily happy. "Labrador," he said. I let him pat her for at least five minutes.

Corky made me sit the emotional curve of slow.

She walked me down a path among hedges and I felt perfect.

If some mornings I'd dark dreams still on my mind, she put shoes in my hands. If I was at a meeting with unkind people, she'd put her paw on my foot, feeling my distress from under the table.

Dogs do these things for nothing. They don't say: "You scratch my back and I'll scratch yours."

Canine empathy doesn't require scales like those held aloft by the goddess of justice. A dog's life is composed minutely of balanced curiosities.

* * *

Many books about service animals suggest they heal wounded people, but this is a bit of a misrepresentation. Disabilities never vanish. What a dog can do is entice you back into the world. That's how a dog thinks of it.

I got it. I was not my dog. My ideas about her were sprinkled over us like a garnish but her instincts, always in my service, were hers.

I knew she loved me but recognized her affection was unrestrainedly alien. Human love is always balloonish, sentimental, but a dog's—well, it's primal, with a pulse, steady. She's asked you in, given you parts of her heart. Some energies she keeps. And her life isn't given to cosseted, overindulgent sweet talk, though she likes it well enough. The mysteries of her love and fast intelligence will never be knowable. I learned to like this as she guided me through streets I couldn't see.

*   *   *

Meanwhile the blind kid still wanted to be liked beyond reason. I felt the highs and lows of service-dog life more keenly than was reasonable. Childhood's demand that I act sighted meant I could easily substitute newer fixations—I imagined for instance I had to be the best guide-dog user ever. I thought I should live so perfectly I'd surpass all others in my appreciation of guide-dog life. Oh and I'd never make mistakes, either in my dog handling or my relations with the public. Of course no one can live like this.

"Real knowledge is to know the extent of one's ignorance," said Confucius. Blind wisdom was grasping what I didn't know, the upside of restriction. "All right," I said, "let's say successful people with disabilities are routinely tested by adversity and in lieu of being bitter (like the classic American victim who appears on TV talk shows) they say instead, we know nothing with the body is what it seems. Wouldn't that be proper conviction?"

*   *   *

The folk singer Greg Brown has a song with the lines: "you come to me with too much laughter / and I teach you how to smile." The song felt true. I didn't want to be so enthusiastic about dog life that I'd pretend by word or deed service dogs are a panacea. In rhetoric there's a term—"proleptic," which means, "the anticipation of possible objections in order to answer them in advance." Living with a guide dog necessitates both knowing and rehearsing how you'll respond to various types of opposition. You're called upon to imagine the bad moments when your difference will be the focus of public attention. My first true experience of this—or the first time I had to put it in action—was in Manhattan. I walked into a large computer store on Sixth Avenue. I wanted to purchase a laptop. As we pushed through the door a security guard put his hand on my chest. "You no come in, no dog," he said.

I pressed forward and the guard stepped back. "Stop! Stop!" he shouted and waved his arms. Customers stared. My civil rights and the security guard's dignity were equally delicate. I didn't know where the guard came from, but his accent sounded East African. How could he possibly know anything about guide dogs? The store's manager hadn't given him information. All he knew was "no dogs allowed," and there I was with a big-assed dog. As we stood in the doorway I figured it would be my job to foster dignity for both of us. They hadn't taught me this at Guiding Eyes; they'd given me a booklet with access laws—a useful thing—I had the right to go anywhere the public went—but no one had mentioned emotional intelligence or how to engage in public mediation.

I made Corky sit. "Listen," I said, softly, "get the manager. This will be okay. This is a special dog for the blind." I wanted to turn our misunderstanding into something respectful.

The manager was one of those guys you see all the time in big-city stores: sadder than his customers, red-faced and put-upon. He had a scoured toughness. He approached and began shouting at the guard. "It's a seeing-eye dog for God's sake! Let him in! Sorry, sorry!"

My fight-or-flee rush was subsiding—I wanted all three of us to experience kindness.

I was in a Manhattan electronics store and dignity was in peril. It would have been easy to say "Fuck it" and look out for myself alone. I'd gotten into the store. I was angry. I could have pitched a fit. But I didn't feel like doing that. The guard's name was Ekwueme. My name was Stephen. The manager's name was Phil. "Listen," I said, "dogs for the blind are not common, you don't see them every day. This is Corky. She's very smart." I let my voice become soft. Ekwueme and Phil both petted Corky. A customer approached, said: "I've raised puppies for the guide-dog school! Best dogs in the world!" Phil seemed suddenly pleased, as if he too was philanthropic, or could be someday. Ekwueme admitted he loved dogs.

Outside with a computer under my arm, I reckoned life with Corky was more complex than just a story of freedom. Ekwueme and Phil would become legion in my travels but I didn't know it yet. What I did know was reflected in a quote I'd always liked from Martin Luther King Jr.: "An individual has not started living until he can rise above the narrow confines of his individualistic concerns to the broader concerns of all humanity."

I sensed that having a service dog meant something more than honoring my own rights. "Take the first step in faith," said Dr. King. "You don't have to see the whole staircase, just take the first step."

*   *   *

Even in the middle of the night Corky was ready for adventure. I felt the lure of the all-night drugstore and we headed through the half-sinister streets of Ithaca in search of vitamins, Mars bars, bubble bath, a styptic pencil. But we were really walking just for the sake of walking. There were no goods we needed to buy.

We entered the twenty-four-hour pharmacy. I swiveled my hips, turning my back to the opened door, to make sure it wouldn't close on Corky's tail, performing the maneuver just as the guide-dog school had taught me. Always protect the tail. Then we were across the threshold, standing in the unforgiving fluorescent light of an average drugstore amid the soaps and ten thousand plastic bottles. Pastel shades assaulted me; there were the odors of newsprint and nail polish. We went up and down the aisles. I didn't want anything. And yet what a curious thing! I liked doing this—just being in a common spot with its useless products was a sort of empiricism. I was awake and grateful in a vulgar commercial space and though I couldn't properly see the products, I toured every corner of the store while praising Corky. No one spoke to me. There were three or four other customers and one cashier. I circled and left.

"You see?" I said, "you've taught me to relish easy things Corky, just a few turns around a drugstore."

"Our life ahead," I thought, "would be about moments of common release—not climbing the Alps but walking an ordinary Walgreens."

It was nice doing what other people did when they couldn't sleep.

Chapter Twenty

Anyone who's waited a long time for a job knows the thoughts you live with. You'll never find another job. Unemployment symbolizes something truly unsavory about you. Even the grass knows it. The supermarket cashier knows you're defective as you give her your food stamps. You'll always be this way. Even sunlight knows you'll never succeed.

Pushing back is hard. You know you've nothing to be ashamed of. So what if you feel mummified? You write between the lines, try to forget pessimism. Not everything is how it appears. I kept telling myself these things.

After fourteen months with Corky I received a telephone call alerting me I was a finalist for a job at Guiding Eyes. On a whim, with no expectation of success, I'd applied for the position of alumni director. I'd imagined they wouldn't be interested in me. For one thing I was still a new guide-dog user who scarcely knew Braille—a necessity for communicating with many blind graduates. Also I hadn't lived through the heartbreak of losing a guide dog, a tragic inevitability in the life of every guide-dog user. I could hardly imagine the pain of such a thing. Who could be strong enough for that? What would happen when the day came to say goodbye to Corky? I'd be reduced to jelly. Finally, I didn't know as much about disability as I thought I should. There were agencies across the country that helped people get back on their feet and I was clueless about them.

In the end they liked me because I was a seasoned public speaker. The president and CEO at the time was a former Manhattan business executive named Bill Badger. Bill was warm and encouraging when I recited what I believed were my drawbacks. "We need someone who can hit the road and talk about what we do," he said. "I think you can help us tell our story."

A man who hadn't known how to walk unfamiliar streets would now find himself in all kinds of places. A superlative village had made this possible, from the kennel staff at Guiding Eyes to puppy raisers; from orientation and mobility professionals to dog trainers. I'd met intensely giving people, those who love dogs and human beings equally. I hadn't met many folks like them before training with Corky. But I knew a good thing when it hit me. In this way I was actually like a trusting dog. I possessed what dog trainers call "recoverability" and realized, owing to all these folks and my dog, I'd never be the same. I'd be more open. I wouldn't be afraid to visit new places. "How," I thought, "can life change so quickly?"

The answer had much to do with the 1990s. Disability culture was blossoming in the wake of the newly ratified Americans with Disabilities Act. Writers and scholars were talking about disability studies—a field where bodily defects were seen to be less significant than long-standing cultural attitudes about them. We were not defective people or "broken" patients, but citizens whose differences are central to society. Along with many writers (whom I later came to know personally) I started addressing disability in my work. Like others I felt discomfort with the way disability is used as a metaphor both in literature and in common language. I read and reread Susan Sontag's *Illness as Metaphor* and began thinking about blindness and figurative language.

Vision loss is always symbolized as abjection, monstrosity, blankness, or death—or it grants compensatory powers of divination, intuition, spiritual grace—neither of which has much to do with real blindness. With

Corky sleeping under my desk I started writing abstruse prose about blindness and symbolism, and it dawned on me I should write something based on my childhood experiences. This approach eventually led me to write my first book, a memoir entitled *Planet of the Blind*.

I set out with Corky on a new passage. I did know one or two things. For instance, losing my provincial teaching job had been a gift—or if not precisely a gift, a forced chance to try something new. How elementary it really had been. They'd sacked me and I'd learned how to walk.

* * *

I was leaving secure little Ithaca, New York, for sub-urban New York. Going through cardboard boxes and old letters I had to admit what a long road I'd been on. Fingering an old set of house keys, I thought of the time I almost died as a teenager—not from blind-ness but depression. At seventeen I stopped eating. I was gravely ill. On the advice of our family doctor (who was concerned but hapless) my parents shipped me to a psychiatric facility in Rochester, New York, an hour's drive from our house, where again no one could unravel my problem. A psychiatrist (who actually had a gray beard) asked if the rawhide lanyard I wore around my neck was a fetish and I knew he was a fool. It was how I wore my house key—a matter any child of alcoholics would understand.

My week in the institute did nothing save that it proved how badly we treat people in advanced suffering. My roommate was an old Ukrainian man covered head to toe with scars. He wept openly. Occasionally he'd ask me to look at him. I'd shuffle over to his bedside and he'd raise his gown and point out his map of scars—most, if not all of them, self-inflicted. He spoke no English.

On my side of the room things were more scientific. A tall medical student put a piece of meat on a string down my throat. He told me they were testing my digestive enzymes. Was I mad or was I a gastrointestinal freak? As with most psychiatric mysteries the good doctors couldn't find a physical answer. They sent me home.

I shook from cold, slept badly. Then one morning, against all odds, I decided to go to church. No one in our family ever went to church.

Skinny. Shaking. Navigating through light and fog. I walked approximately five hundred yards to the Episcopal chapel at Hobart and William Smith Colleges.

I'd never been there. I went in.

There were perhaps twenty professors and their wives sitting in the pews. I knew some of them vaguely from faculty events at our home. They were peculiar adults, slightly troubling, as they knew who I was. Appearing alone in the chapel would I be remarked upon?

I sat. Closed my eyes. I was dizzy. Hunger does that of course, but being in public, in a church, sitting in a sunbeam, that also makes you spin. I was killing myself. I knew it, somehow, in the clotted way teenagers know things. I both did and did not want to go on.

My blindness was a problem. Certainly I was the reason my mother drank and took pills. Surely my ruined eyes were the source of her despair. Surely if I was just a better child, less defective, or more successful at covering up my deficiencies, why then all would be better.

My frail shoulders carried that weight. I was seventeen and already an old man.

An Episcopal bishop from Rochester spoke. He was kindly and had the same warmth as the sunlight, which my face was absorbing rather desperately.

Next came a bell. We'd entered the Eucharist, about which I knew nothing. I was shivering in a church pew.

I went to the altar rail, got down on my knees, reached out and took the bread. "Take and eat, for this is my body." It was the sacrament of Christ's flesh and blood. My fingers were anemic as I took the bread, and my hands shook. "Come, risen Lord, and deign to be our guest . . ." "My God, thy table now is spread . . ." "I am the bread of life . . ."

"Do this in remembrance of me . . ." How could I explain . . . certainly I was a starving blind adolescent, chilled in April light, one foot from death; who felt a heat inside, who felt his own blood and flesh kissed from somewhere deep and still. Do this in remembrance of me. Eat, consecrate your mortal flesh.

I decided to live from that day forward. I never mentioned the experience to anyone.

Maybe I didn't know how to talk about the death of a guide dog but I'd been schooled in losing and gaining hope. I put the old house keys in the "kept things box"—the keys that once hung from a lanyard. I knew the boy who once was me was evermore part of the grown man who came late to walking free.

Chapter Twenty-One

Traveling the country talking about guide dogs brought both the austerities and dignities of disability into focus. Meeting each month's class of guide-dog students taught me innumerable and astonishing things. I hadn't known diabetes was the number one cause of blindness in the United States. As soon as I started working at Guiding Eyes I met a woman named Janice who, owing to diabetes, had lost all feeling in both her feet and was fighting to stay alive. Trainers paired her with a petite yellow Lab named Maisie who was exceedingly careful when observing and reacting to terrain—Maisie helped compensate for Janice's inability to feel the ground. They were so artful together.

Janice went home with Maisie only to die from diabetes a few months later. I wrote in my journal: *live now; Lord, don't let us forget to live now . . .*

Every day I saw no two blind people are alike. I met a deaf-blind college student named Eric who lost both his sight and hearing from Usher syndrome. He communicated by typing and typed for me his assessment of Braille. "Braille saved my life," he said. "It's the number one communication tool for deaf-blind people; but man, you spend your life reading it and it's like you're always rubbing a plucked chicken."

People faced depression, PTSD, high blood pressure, anxiety, balance problems, multiple sclerosis, brain injuries, and traumas without names. In the disability-rights community many hate the word *inspiration* since it hearkens back to Charles Dickens's Tiny Tim or Jerry Lewis. We hope to live without being inspirational. But I watched Ronald, who was both legally blind and had cerebral palsy, working his dog, swaying and pivoting with each step, his black Labrador adjusting, actually dancing alongside him. Several guide-dog schools told Ronald he couldn't get a dog but Guiding Eyes said yes. Seeing him work his sleek black Labrador was "righteous"—something better than inspiration.

I saw students fight step by step, not merely for mobility but for the tenor of life, the reason we live. As one of my favorite poets, William Stafford, said: "From human loss, from gravel, from stone, after years, one holds what one can."

Hannah was from Boston and had a wonderful,

hard laugh. She also had an environmental disability. She was severely allergic to chemicals. Everyone in the training class had to avoid using aftershaves and perfumes. The custodial staff had to find chemical-free products. Talking daily with her I saw how precarious her situation was. "I'm like a tightrope walker," she said, "but who'd pay to see my circus?"

"Well, I don't know," I said, "but you should patent the idea of a chemical-free circus right away. Its day will come."

"The only animals would be hypoallergenic poodles," she said. We imagined poodles jumping through flaming hoops. But joking aside, Hannah could turn scarlet and fight for breath if she encountered the wrong environment. Entering the perfume section in a department store was terrifying for her. But she could laugh—it was one of her talents. "I'm the world's greatest respiratory diva," she said.

* * *

Working at a guide-dog school required a role reversal for me. Teaching courses in college had meant I was an authority. Now I was learning things that were entirely new. I was in the process of admitting all the things about blindness and guide dogs that I didn't know. For instance, I never knew there were advocacy groups by and for the blind that didn't agree with each other; one group argued for tactile warning strips in subway stations while another thought this was demeaning to the blind. One organization preferred white-cane travel over guide dogs. Blind politics could be intense. I had difficulty understanding some of this—not from a partisan perspective—but because I'd always understood individualism depends on personal choice. Some blind activists liked talking street signs. Others believed they were unnecessary. "If they're unnecessary," I thought, "how could they be harmful to those who don't like them?" The anti-talking-street-sign contingent felt that the public, seeing such a thing, might perceive the blind as vaguely helpless. Orientation and mobility skills should obviate the need for any assistive device. I discovered that factions evinced the same passions one sees among football fans. I made some notes. I really wanted to resist puritanism whenever possible.

* * *

Mostly I learned by listening. Some evenings I sat with students and we'd talk about disability in America. I met people with graduate degrees who couldn't get past initial job interviews. "Once they discover you're blind they don't call you back for a second interview," said Jack, who had two Ivy League degrees. Another student described the miserable state of public transportation in his town. If you live outside a major city the chances are excellent the blind can't even get to a job. "It's hard enough being disabled," he said, "but then they stack everything else against you. At least with my dog I can take good walks to relieve the frustration."

"You're only as independent as the infrastructure allows," said Jason, a playwright from Manhattan. "If trains run on time; if the taxi stops for you; if a bus driver calls out the stops. Without these things you can be erased."

* * *

Some students had attended schools for the blind, at least for a time, and had advantages over those who'd gone to public schools without proper support. The blind-school graduates were crackerjack Braille readers. Many also had a far better sense that blindness is an element of life and nothing very special. Regardless of our respective backgrounds we found we hadn't met enough other blind people. If you came from a small town chances were good you'd never met a blind person. Talking offered proof that we were quick, true, patient, and bold.

* * *

The ADA makes it clear what the term "disability" means with respect to an individual: *(A) a physical or mental impairment that substantially limits one or more major life activities of such individual, (B) a record of such an impairment or (C) being regarded as having such an impairment.*

Major life activities include but are not limited to: *caring for oneself, performing manual tasks, seeing, hearing, eating, sleeping, walking, standing, lifting, bending, speaking, breathing, learning, reading, concentrating, thinking, communicating, and working.*

Major bodily functions means: *functions of the immune system, normal cell growth, digestive, bowel, bladder, neurological, brain, respiratory, circulatory, endocrine, and reproductive functions.*

The range of disability is wide. Talking about obstacles, especially where jobs were concerned, I understood Americans confuse the ability to perform major life functions with accomplishment. In turn the disabled are thought to lack every kind of competency. This I thought must be why some believe guide dogs make decisions for the blind. People think the dogs do everything since obviously blindness means we can't think.

"This function disjunction affects all the disabled," I thought. "Wheelchair users and the deaf are also thought to be helpless."

"It's a tough world. There are plenty of bad ideas still circulating," I said to Jason one night over pizza.

"The trick is," said Jason, "to grow out of them. I mean you were a blind kid yourself, and even so, with all your personal experience you had tons of shitty ideas about disability."

"No question," I said.

*   *   *

Older dog handlers—students returning to school for their fifth or sixth dog—had lived much of their lives before the ADA, when the blind and their allies fought for inclusion state by state. Between the 1940s and the 1970s blind activists fought vigorously for the rights of white-cane users and guide-dog teams. Marjorie, a student training with her fifth dog, told me that when she received her first dog in the early 1960s the white cane and the guide dog were still not fully understood.

She explained that the white cane was introduced in the US by the Lions Club in Peoria in the 1930s. The art of sweeping the cane from side to side for detection didn't come until a pioneering orientation specialist named Richard Hoover introduced the technique almost ten years later, in the mid 1940s. The cane began to have wide use. It became universally white to alert motorists its owner was blind. With this breakthrough the cane was transformed into an effective mobility device.

She explained that just as white-cane laws mandating drivers yield to the blind were being adopted, guide-dog accessibility also became a matter of law.

"Finally in October of 1964," Marjorie said, "Lyndon Johnson signed a proclamation declaring White Cane Safety Day."

"So if you think about it," said Marjorie, "our nation's recognition of blind independence is still in its infancy." Then she laughed. "And to think I got my first dog in the era of Patty Duke and *The Miracle Worker*. No one thought blind people were supposed to leave the asylum," she said. "And there I'd go, a young woman, just a girl really, with a German shepherd, and we were in Woolworths, and all hell would break loose. *Miss, you can't come in here with that animal* . . . you know, the manager . . . and then Darlene, the woman who worked the luncheonette, said . . . *Oh Carl shut up, can't you see that's one of those blind-dogs?* And they argued for a minute or two but I just went to the back of the store where they kept the dog toys. That was always a good technique, to keep moving and let them argue about the dog."

We talked about how there's a service dog for almost any disability now . . . dogs assist wheelchair users, open cupboards, hand money to cashiers or help people with balance . . . or they detect the onset of seizures. They alert the deaf to critical sounds . . . They even assist diabetics by sensing changes in blood sugar.

We talked about how all those skills reflect the limitless talents of dogs and the pioneering work of the guide-dog movement, which began the service-dog industry so many years ago.

"But here's what I think," I said to Marjorie. "Despite the advantages of working dogs, many who rely on them still experience problems—just as you did in 1963 . . ."

Lately stories had been piling up on my desk—a veteran and his service dog had been recently booted out of a fast food restaurant; another vet was denied access on a public bus. A legally blind woman was hassled in a movie theater by a customer who said that she and her dog were fakes.

Marjorie had worked for years in the rehabilitation field. I asked her what she thought could be done.

"Some argue these problems could be prevented by requiring service-dog users to carry identification cards," she said, "but there's a good reason we don't want to do this—my disability is my business and not yours."

"Yes," I said, "the easiest way to tell if a dog is working is by its professionalism. And business owners are not forced to admit or endure misbehaving dogs. In fact it's the performance of a service dog that really matters— not just in traffic or in crowds, but everywhere."

Inevitably we began to talk about nondisabled people who pretend to have disabilities just to take their dogs anywhere they go.

"Then you come along with your authentic guide dog and they want you to prove you're blind," Marjorie said.

"Nowadays people imagine there are disability advantages like better parking or early boarding on airplanes. Did you ever think you'd live to see disability as a preferred lifestyle?" I asked.

"Nope," she said, "but the current scene is a whole lot better than the old one."

"Which old one?" I said.

"Well, there were the ugly laws in the United States," she told me. "In the nineteenth and even the early twentieth century people with disabilities were outlawed from appearing on the streets in many municipalities."

Thinking about this was chilling.

* * *

Problems aside, every month's class was really about love. Nothing in my college experience prepared me for this. What do you call a love collective featuring dogs and blind people? Did it matter if there was no term for it? Sometimes walking a hallway with Corky I'd hear singing from a dorm room. Women sang to their dogs and so did men. Love was palpable. Dogs were deciding to accept new people in room after room. The dogs weren't merely giving their new owners the benefit of the doubt, they were giving them their faith. Dogs can tell when your heart is open—can tell when you're dignifying them with your trust. Dogs smell trust.

Chapter Twenty-Two

What I knew about love I could put in a thimble. It was akin to my knowledge of "red," for what did I know about it? I knew it was an important color.

"Love," I thought, "is for other people."

I'd lived a long time thinking this way.

In 1961 my mother constructed a bomb shelter under our house and filled it with canned goods and jars of water. I went there whenever I was roughed up by neighboring children. I lay on cool cement and whispered stories to no one. That's how my stories unfolded, talking in the dark, breathing the odor of army blankets. Who loves you, who doesn't, where's a lucky window, how high the sun, my lips moving. Yes, love was for others until I met Connie and I met Connie because of her dog, Roscoe, who was absolutely wild about Corky.

One morning I followed Corky up a flight of stairs to see what it was she wanted. And up those stairs where the admissions office of the guide-dog school was located was a black dog, a hilarious dog. Some dogs are genuinely funnier than others and some are smart about it, and Roscoe was a Labrador comedian. And like all comics he was a dropout. He'd flunked out of guide-dog school as a puppy. He'd been bred to be a working dog but he ran off at the sound of shaken coins in a can. This meant he was sound-shy, which automatically disqualified him from guide-dog work. But he made up for it with a remarkable fun index. He bounced at the sight of Corky and whirled and said, "I'm here, I'm here!" He was tall, loose jointed, his big tongue out, tail wagging, and Corky jumped as if a door had opened right before her.

That's how it is when you fall in love—dogs know it without waffling. Corky was in love and since fathomless things happen against expectation soon I was in love.

* * *

I was forty and walking straight into a love story written by Labradors. I met Connie, a former guide-dog trainer who ran the admissions office, who had one of the loveliest voices I'd ever heard, who I'd find by and by was very beautiful—for I require scientific closeness to see anything, perhaps one may say indecently close, or better yet, lovingly near. But I wasn't there yet—still, yes, she had a voice and a love of dogs and curiosity about both animals and people, and that ain't ipso facto, not customary, though we wish it would be, for it's an ancient sensibility. Soon Connie and I and Roscoe and Corky were taking walks.

I wondered how one might tell this tale.

Dear X:

I could be falling in love with my dog's best friend-dog's owner. I'm middle-aged and holding hands with Connie. I'm laughing. I tell her about birdcalls. Tell her grackles sound like reeds. I've fallen in love with my dog's best friend-dog's owner . . . We walk on a long, abandoned rail line. The dogs say "this this this" and run the curves of a tree line; the dogs say we've all come perfectly together . . .

The sun comes out from behind the clouds. I'm in love. I tell Connie about the red-winged blackbirds. My dog's dog-friend's owner is beautiful.

* * *

Yes, red was an important color. So was morning blue. We walked beside a lake and I don't remember the name of it now, but we were laughing like hell. Laughing just because one can. Because I told Connie she looked like a Phrygian goddess and then was forced to admit all women look like goddesses when you're blind and so what? Yes, we laughed. We agreed: if everyone looks good there's no need for praise. What a relief! And then no need for heroes! Laugh more. Run in circles like Roscoe who has a five-foot-long stick in his mouth. It's more than a stick, it's a branch, and he knows it's the most important thing in the world, a birch limb tasting of yeast and don't you wish you had one? And you should talk less, really, and just chase me.

* * *

I didn't know much. Not just about love. I was still coming into the world in a late rebirth having decided to cross streets, kick up dust the way the sighted do—a phrase I'd stolen from a national advocacy group which was always saying the blind could do customary things, read newspapers, for instance, "just like visual people do." Now I was making my forays into Manhattan or a hundred other precincts just as the sighted did, and yet, hell, I didn't know much. I had no idea how to be in love. Did you enter it with a processional march as in

Verdi's *Aida*, or was it just an earnest little tune picked out on a homely banjo? Was there a song at all? Did you make up your mind to be in love?

No, you didn't. You didn't make up your mind at all. Not if the dogs were right.

* * *

I'd imagined no love was going to be my lot. I simply knew I was defective. The nondefective people held parties, danced, made plans. Space opened for them. They didn't have to question it. Every place was theirs and all that American materiality was theirs—their cars with rag tops; trips to the beach. That's how it felt, anyway. The no-love narrative was basically stupid. It was no better than thinking the man in the moon was a beggar who collects sticks on Sundays—a mythology people long believed—yes, stupid, but if you live a provincial life you can be convinced of anything.

Sudden love is to be unconvinced. And the irony, the loveliest of them, the most statuesque irony of them all, is I got there by walking, thrilling to moments, trusting open air, taking Connie and my dog to the opera. During intermission, as we sipped champagne and Corky sat trimly beside us, a woman said:

"Who's your dog's favorite composer?" and I said, "Puccini, of course."

How long can you say you know nothing about love? I had to give it away just as dogs give small things away throughout the day. "Oh for Chrissake," say the dogs, "let's run over here. Let's together put our noses in these leaves."

* * *

Connie and I were in love rather quickly and I'll never not believe it was Roscoe and Corky's doing. We didn't take a chance. We didn't have to. We knew we could trust our dogs. Not because it made for a story. But because there it was, we fit.

This "fit" involved a man, a woman, two dogs, and two children. Connie was a single mom and along came Tara, age eight, and Ross, six. We sang Pete Seeger's song, "All Around the Kitchen" and hurtled around Connie's house shouting "cocka-doodle-doo" while the dogs approved and crockery rattled.

Sometimes we lay on the floor, Tara, Ross, Connie, and I, and the dogs took up the business of washing our faces as their ropy tails knocked knickknacks off tables.

*   *   *

Labradors are not fast runners but Roscoe was very quick. He was an acrobat and a superb Frisbee catcher. No matter the falling angle, no matter how bad the throw, he'd yank a Frisbee out of the air, sometimes with a shoestring catch just before it hit the ground. And Corky, who was slow, would turn to her boy and bounce around him. If Roscoe wasn't alert Corky would grab his prize and tug-of-war would ensue. Many a Frisbee met an early demise.

Corky and Roscoe were in love, that red, warm-blooded enthrallment of dogs in each other's company.

Chapter Twenty-Three

Corky and I hit the road over the next five years. My primary goal was to talk about dogs for the blind. I spoke at state fairs, union halls, schools, rehab agencies, conferences, and various charity galas. We would visit forty-seven states and three foreign countries. Some weeks it seemed as if we were in perpetual motion. Arriving in each city, Corky went bounding up the Jetway as if eager to explore the unknown (in reality she was thrilled to get off the plane where she'd had to curl up under my feet.)

Our flights were sometimes beautiful and periodically strange. Disabled people never know how a plane flight is going to go. Not all flight attendants are trained to serve disabled passengers. Cabin personnel are like the rest of us—overtaxed, working to their limit. For some the sight of a Labrador boarding a plane brightens everything. After settling Corky at my feet I'd listen to their stories—told quickly—of the dogs they'd left behind and couldn't wait to see. Corky made a lot of airline employees smile.

But things could quickly turn strange. Boarding a flight to Wisconsin, where I was to speak at a conference on blindness and rehabilitation, the flight attendant said: "That dog doesn't have a blue blanket, it can't come on the plane." Standing in the aircraft's doorway I was momentarily flummoxed.

"Guide dogs don't have blue blankets," I said. "I'm not sure what you mean."

"Oh no," she said. "That dog has to have a blue blanket or it can't come on the plane."

"You know," I said, "when guide dogs are in training as puppies they wear blue blankets, maybe that's what you're thinking of?"

"I don't know," she said. "But you can't come on this plane."

Civil rights veterans know the next trick. You just sit down. I sat in the nearest seat. I tucked Corky under my feet.

"You'll have to get a supervisor," I said.

She stormed off the plane and up the Jetway. Civilization had stopped. People with oversize bags piled onto the aircraft without a flight attendant.

When the attendant reappeared she said nothing. Someone had obviously told her it was okay. Her silence suggested she'd been humiliated or patronized by a superior.

This lack of training was something we faced consistently. We never knew when we'd have a blue-blanket moment. On a flight from Portland, Oregon, to New York I was given an inaccessible seat. It was in the middle of a three-seat row, where I discovered metal stanchions, which, in turn, made it impossible to get Corky safely under the seat. Then the attendant put two people on either side of me. She asked me to get up so a passenger could get to the window seat. I had to get Corky back into the aisle. Boarding passengers wouldn't make way for us in the aisle. That's when my dog decided she wouldn't go back to our designated spot. I told the attendant she should reseat us where we could actually sit. She looked at me as if I might be half human. The plane was a Boeing 757, which meant the bulkhead seats were in an exit row. "People with disabilities are barred from sitting in an exit row, sir!" she said. "And first class is full, sir!" she added. I told her under the Air Carrier Access Act our right to fly safely and in comfort is not up for grabs and she stomped off, leaving us in the aisle, only to return with the captain, who wisely moved us to the front of the plane where there was more room. The dismissiveness of the flight attendant was hard to fathom.

* * *

I never knew what would happen while traveling but I was doing what I'd said I wanted—going to unknown cities. Poor treatment from airlines meant little compared to the surprises and new friendships that happened. Soon after joining Guiding Eyes I took a trip to Monterey, California, to speak about guide dogs at a regional conference. There I met Michael Meteyer, one of America's most highly regarded orientation-and-mobility specialists. I was making my way down the street with Corky, searching for coffee, when Michael called out, having recognized me from a poster. Though we'd never met it quickly seemed we'd always known each other: his mother was blind and he helped her while growing up. He saw early that blindness is ordinary. He went on to attend the University of Rochester, just an hour west of Geneva. Like me he was a student of poetry and had taken courses with one of my favorite poets, Anthony Hecht. When he left college he met Lawrence Ferlinghetti and rode horses with him daily. We sat in a café not far from

John Steinbeck's "Cannery Row" and talked about poetry, disability, and animals.

It didn't take long before we were speculating about animal souls. Are dogs meant to bring us together? The café smelled of bread and coffee. The moment was poignant. Michael had played football for the University of Rochester while I was in the psychiatric hospital just five miles away. After college he'd gone far, helping the blind in Africa, traveling in America's Deep South, ultimately moving to California. His life was about travel and affirmation—especially where the blind are concerned. Had I been destined to meet him? Was this Corky's plan?

* * *

In one of his notebooks Leonardo da Vinci wrote: "Man has great power of speech, but the greater part thereof is empty and deceitful. The animals have little, but that little is useful and true; and better is a small and certain thing than a great falsehood." Da Vinci was correct about human speech and deceit, and nearly right about animals having a truer language, but he couldn't have guessed how much truth and courage the animals have. I was living it.

In San Francisco, down by Fisherman's Wharf, it sank in—bonding with a guide was a walking prayer without the need for nonsecular miracles. Two years prior I'd said the words "I need to walk." I thought, "Truth, faith . . ." Script and scripture. The little that is useful and true on my dog.

I sat with Corky and listened to sea lions. The sea lions were haughty and loud. The boy still inside me wanted to run down the wharf waving his arms. The blind boy had always been good at running wildly. The grown man understood this joy. The man and dog understood. The man and dog and boy got up together and covered the long wharf with very fast footfalls.

*   *   *

The cities were lovely.

Early on the street. Name the city. Houston.

We walked in a neighborhood of Victorian houses. The morning was quiet. Then, through an open window, I heard someone playing Franz Liszt's "Hungarian Rhapsody No. 2." It was better for being clumsy—sweet in the strangeness of a city where we were foreign.

Visiting the Highbanks Metro Park in Columbus,

Ohio, where cliffs overlook the Olentangy River, Corky scented muskrats and I smelled wet shale.

In the Fairchild Tropical Botanic Garden in Miami, Florida, we walked through the rare plant house smelling cycads, ferns, orchids, aroids, bromeliads, fruit trees, and vines thick as legs.

We walked the Packery Channel Park in Corpus Christi, Texas, where the ocean smelled of brine and, oddly, of pineapple. I was convinced the bay was filled with fruit juice. I was certain that Corky could smell the sandhill cranes.

Particulate odors. Shambling in space.

Fences, trees, oleander, stray hedgehogs.

The poems of her nose!

Mice; synthetic dyes; odors of human wrists . . .

Five a.m. in Jackson, Mississippi. Corky did her morning business and I heard two men, far off, laughing in mutual, unvexed joy. It was the best two-man laugh I'd ever heard.

In my notebook I wrote: *Think of a dog's language. It's ours of course—ball, rope, shoe. But for dogs there are proto-signs, dog signs, liquid, quick as sparrows in grass. I think dogs had words before they met us. For "grouse" they may have something damp, for dogs feel their words.*

* * *

Boarding a plane I wondered what her nouns signified. On the commuter Dash 8 aircraft flying to Buffalo did she sense the odors of fish bladders and wet feathers? Did she smell human fear? What did she understand of the upright figures staring at magazines with their stink of linens and apples? She lay at my feet and I thought while dogs don't have preceptive nouns they've a canine genome—which in turn means they've a long, hieratic dictionary of meanings. Many a flight was more interesting for this.

* * *

I had many odd excursions. At a conference in Ohio, as I was wrapping up a speech about the benefits of guide dogs, a woman handed me an envelope. "Have someone read this to you," she whispered.

Later in the parking lot I showed the letter to Connie. She read it. The woman wanted to bequeath me her son's eyes.

"You'll know what to do with them," she wrote.

Her son was twenty. He had a developmental disability. He couldn't speak.

"He won't be long for this world," she said. "I want his eyes to go to you.

"I've been watching you. I think you're worthy," she said.

It gave me "the fantods," as Huck Finn would say. I was chilled to my core.

My speech had been about dignity. Our wishes for others may or may not be received as we hope. "Maybe I'd be less surprised if I'd been more of a traveler in my teens and twenties," I said to Connie. One characteristic of my new worldliness was my easy bewilderment meeting peculiar people. The world isn't what we think it is.

In Raleigh, North Carolina, I spoke about the role wounded warriors have played advancing the rights of the disabled. Troops return from every war to change the world by insisting on inclusion. Somehow a man in the audience heard something different. He approached me. He shouted. He'd heard me talking about Vietnam vets and decided I was a war protestor. He was not to be dissuaded. As he yelled Corky stood and got between us. She wasn't trained to protect me. But she inserted her big body and stood tall. A hotel security officer appeared and gently led the man away saying: "It's okay, how about a cup of coffee? Let's go get a cup." Maybe he was a veteran with PTSD. I'd never know. I was half dazed and felt the urge to cry in the foyer of the Marriott Hotel.

* * *

We traveled because guide-dog schools are not as well known as they should be. There are approximately a dozen guide schools in the United States. All the schools are nonprofit organizations. They receive no federal or state money and rely exclusively on donations. While American guide-dog schools aren't staggeringly wealthy, they are able, by and large, with the help of their donors, to provide expensive services to a clientele that's not generally well-off. Guide dogs are provided free of charge. Despite this, many people don't know about their programs. One reason for this is the sheer size of America. Not only is the United States a vast country, it's decentralized and largely rural. Learning about disability services is hit or miss. "A patient comes in for an eye exam," an ophthalmologist at the University of Iowa once told me, "and the doctor says, 'Well, you're losing your sight and there's nothing more we can do for you. You better hand over your car keys.' And the patient goes home to Ottumwa and never comes back. He lives in a trailer behind the family farmhouse. People don't learn there are opportunities for the blind."

Talking about dogs was an almost evangelical thing for me. I'd go almost anywhere. One evening I spoke to a 4H club in a small town near Buffalo, New York. My audience was mostly teenagers. Their parents wore feed caps and drank coffee. I quoted the poet Mark Van Doren: "There is one thing we can do, and the happiest people are those who can do it to the limit of their ability. We can be completely present. We can be all here. We can give all our attention to the opportunity before us." "This is the thing," I said, "you give everything to raising a guide-dog puppy, but the *everything* comes from your spirit—it's your happiness, your wakefulness, your love of life itself. Puppies take this into their hearts like vitamins.

"Then one day a blind person goes into the world and your puppy, now a guide dog, shares your happiness, wakefulness, love—shares it by being completely present.

"I know," I told them, "I sound a little like my Finnish grandfather who was a Lutheran minister.

"We can be all here," I said again. I let Corky out of

223

her harness and she went all around the room visiting each person one by one. (She'd actually do that.)

After the warmth of my grange-hall visit I woke later that night in our motel room—a motel that was just down the road from a prison—and I heard weeping through the heat ducts. Corky and I lay in bed and listened to an inconsolable woman crying just a room away. She wept all night. Lying awake, hearing her grief, this too was being present. There are many hard places in America. Could a person from this town reliably find her way to a guide dog? Or any kind of social services? "It's nice to feel loved," I said to Corky. "It's nice to insist on it for others."

Chapter Twenty-Four

Connie had been a guide-dog trainer before taking over the admissions program at Guiding Eyes. We talked a lot about dogs—about what they know and how sharp they are. Dogs never forget a thing. She told me about how she and some other trainers used to stop every day while training dogs to get coffee at a place that was primarily a dirty bookstore. Later when the dogs were paired with students, one Labrador in particular insisted on dragging her blind owner into the shop. "Every day," Connie said, "we'd have to stop and I'd say, *I don't know why he likes it here . . . really . . . I swear . . .*"

She told me about training a dog and needing to use a restroom. She was in Manhattan working a Labrador named John. They went together into a bathroom stall. Connie kept saying: "Down, John, John no! Stay John . . ." There was a woman in the next toilet, she said, "who was flabbergasted."

I wanted Connie's take on the public—that is, when training a guide dog you're essentially a sighted person playing at being blind. Often the public doesn't know the difference.

"Sometimes," I said, "I'm walking and I know someone is staring at me. It's palpable. Did you experience this when you were training dogs?"

"All the time," Connie said. "There are lascivious men who look you up and down. Because they think you're blind they take another look and then another. That's when I'd just stop the training and stare them down. They'd panic then, turn red, and run away."

"Then of course there are those looks of pity—it's always intolerable—the *poor blind person* look."

"Sometimes," she said, "I'd like to put a portable camera on my head and record the able-bodied . . . I'd just walk around in the role of a blind traveler. Then I'd confront the starers, like *Candid Camera . . .*"

"I like it," I said.

* * *

Guide-dog trainers always play the role of blindness. The nature of their job is to train a dog so soundly that the trainer, wearing a blindfold, can walk that dog in heavy traffic. They will trust the dog while walking down subway stairs in the Bronx. They'll commit their own safety to the dogs they've trained. Blindfolded you can't second-guess a dog. The hours spent praising and encouraging a dog's confidence are rewarded. That spritely Labrador who you thought might fail because at first she was silly has become a take-charge girl, and because you can't peel back the blindfold you have to trust her. Below ground in the 138th Street–Grand Concourse station you know she's ready to work. You didn't surmise it, you felt it while you moved in pitch blackness beside a railway platform.

Sometimes you wear occluders, spectacles designed to minimize vision. You see only silver light and shadows. You work a string of dogs—six dogs most days—up and down flights of stairs in a shopping mall. Training dogs, you relinquish some parts of yourself at moments. Confident dogs must know they're helping you.

There's no job quite like it. It doesn't pay well. You go through a long apprenticeship to gain your place, starting out performing manual labor in kennels, then looking after the dogs of senior trainers, following those trainers, sitting in on classes with the blind, wearing a blindfold for weeks while feeling your way around the training center. You experience helplessness, vague humiliations, tears, occasional danger, extremes of weather.

Trainers get the kind of sports injuries known to runners and tennis players—repetitive stress, knee problems, fasciitis, joint inflammation. They work in all weather. Connie told me about wearing a blindfold and working a dog in heavy rain. The roar of water from passing cars robs you of your sense of traffic; you can't tell where it's coming from. It was one of Connie's first blindfolded outings. "Right away I understood," she said. "I was going to trust this dog. And I wasn't going to let her know I was fearful."

It wasn't until I worked at Guiding Eyes that I understood how much the trainers endure. Most trainers are introverts. They're not natural talkers—you might say they're outdoorsy strong, silent types. They're generally not boastful. One trainer told me over breakfast early on a winter's morning, "What we do isn't much, hell it's not even interesting, we get the dogs to go in a line, we get them to stop. We teach them to trust their own instincts. Give them some lingo. It's the dogs who do the work."

I didn't believe a word he said. But I knew why he said it. We all face a choice between freedom and grief. The former requires not thinking so much of yourself

you forget what road you're on. Modesty is a require-
ment if you're walking a long way.

*   *   *

What do dogs really think of us? All kinds of people
asked me this, so I had to think about it often. Who
presumes to speak for all dogs? I couldn't even speak
for blind people, how could I generalize about Corky
or any other dog? I realized dogs would be a fascination
for me but one I'd never get to the bottom of. Admitting what I didn't know about dogs meant I had to be
both ironic and skeptical. Some dogs are smarter than
others. Guide dogs tend to be Renaissance types—dogs
capable of doing many things. As Brian Hare, the famous canine cognition researcher at Duke University
points out, Renaissance dogs show flexibility across five
cognitive dimensions: empathy, communication, cunning, memory, and reasoning. Guide-dog trainers, the
best ones, the ones whose dogs succeed most often,
know that these five qualities are characteristics of the
dog and not the man or woman who trains it. The job
is to bring these capacities out. "It's a bit like Michelangelo carving the *Pietà*," Kylie, my trainer with Corky,

said to me one day. "The dog emerges from a block of marble. Maybe the marble was excellent to begin with. The Guiding Eyes breeding center has a lot to do with that. But we're giving dogs the opportunity to thrive."

Corky: Empathy. Check. Communication: sure. Cunning. A great word. Achieving one's ends by deceit or diversion. Would deceit be a good quality for a guide dog? No. But every dog has some deceitful qualities. Guide-dog users must know what to do when their dogs want them to enter a hedge because there's a rabbit down by the roots. A duplicitous dog is a thinking creature. Now you have to be in charge.

Memory. Certainly. Reasoning. Absolutely. When a guide dog takes you around an open construction site, carefully working her way off the sidewalk, looking for the right path back to safety, that's reasoning par excellence.

It became a kind of gift I could give back to Corky, to say I couldn't quite get to the bottom of what she thought. Her life was elusive.

Connie and I agreed dogs make us more human.

Working at a guide-dog school one gets to see it every day. There's a gruff student, an older man; he's gone blind late in life, he's angry. When he speaks he's basically monosyllabic. When he's introduced to his new dog he talks to it robotically. His words are like little needle points. And his dog, who's used to praise, well the dog wonders what's up. She looks at the man frequently, and her expression is inquiring. Then the unknown beautiful happens—it can't be explained—the man warms, laughs, by week two he actually laughs.

Something inside the man, some wheel, broke under its own weight. The trainer sees: it was the dog who did it. The Renaissance dog knows she can outlast the man. How does she know? She just does.

Chapter Twenty-Five

After five years at Guiding Eyes I returned to teaching. Connie and the kids and I moved to Columbus, Ohio, where I took a job teaching creative writing and disability studies at Ohio State.

"The only perk to being blind is you can take your dog anywhere," I said to students when I entered the classroom. Teaching with a guide dog was glorious. It wasn't just the shtick of the thing—as when students were quiet and I'd say, "Well Corky knows the answer . . ." It was really the case that for the first time in my academic life I felt even-tempered. Silence was good. I didn't have to fill gaps in conversation. And if a student was distressed he or she could have a dog-petting session. Higher education can be painful, steeped in competition; often students struggle without evident maps. "Another natural place for dogs," I thought.

We learn best when we're safe, when we feel intimacy with ideas. We don't learn well with arbitrary pressure and force. When dogs stare into our eyes, releasing in us oxytocin, the bonding hormone—Lord knows, our pulse rates drop, our breathing steadies.

The whole room changes for the better when a large dog lying outstretched decides halfway through the allotted period to put her four feet in the air and waggle them. Even the fluorescent lights in a cheap university classroom won't bother you. A dog in class insists love and compassion are necessities, not luxuries. Love may be the hardest thing to put into action, but after each class I encouraged my students to visit with Corky.

* * *

A guide dog taught me to live wisely. She did it every day of her thirteen years. After she died I sat in my backyard with her ashes. I cradled her urn in my lap. "What," I thought, "would she want to teach me now?

"She'd want me to trust what's ahead," I thought. She'd want me to live in the now. She'd certainly want me to be happy and never give up on love.

"Courage," said Hemingway, "is grace under pressure." I'd never felt like an especially courageous person. But in the veterinary clinic as she was breathing her last I knew quite clearly Corky had spent her life protecting me. She always looked out for me, my special angel.

I knew I had to force back my tears because I couldn't let her die to the sounds of my distress. I lay beside her, held her, and sang for her our special walking song. And she died in my arms.

One day your dog is with you, a keen physical presence. She stands under lilac bushes as reliable as always. The next day she's gone. She becomes, finally, something of you. Every death is just so. We look for consolation. We falter. With grace we're turned and loss is yet another segment of our path.

Corky's spirit was never my sole possession. She wasn't me. She was never mine. She was wisdom's passing gift.

She wrote commentaries on my sad and sometimes joyous frame, wrote them as only a dog could with her translating eyes and prophesying gait.

After Corky passed I thought hard about my transformation. She brought it the same way she brought my shoes each morning. She'd rise from her bed and retrieve my Nikes. Shoes first, then the glorious day, always a dog's suggestion.

Afterword

In writing about guide-dog travel I've tried to portray both the freedom a dog can bring as well as the occasional misunderstandings service-dog users encounter. The latter are much like anything else—obstructive things happen but they're infrequent. A cursory reading may lend one to imagine every day is filled with roadblocks when you have a guide dog. In fact most days are expansive and inviting. Walking with a professionally trained dog is a magnificent way to travel. Though I've had a few bad taxi rides, the majority of cabbies are terrific. Once, outside of Macy's flagship store in New York a cab driver told me his sister in Cairo was deaf. He was putting in long hours, saving his money to bring her to the United States. "People here understand disability," he said. Corky was sitting tall and looking at him. He asked if he could pet her and I said yes. He stroked her ears. I knew he was silently telling her to keep up the good work.

Disability is a Victorian word, strange as "antimacassar" or "corset," and just so, you shouldn't rest your head there or wrap yourself in a pejorative meaning. A disabled life is as stimulating as any other. That disablement and blindness sometimes have social barriers is a fact. A shopkeeper may not understand a guide dog, but generally such people are educable and the problem is minor.

Why mention stumbling blocks at all? In part I've done so because service dogs are an increasingly important accommodation and I want to convey my sense that as the organized training of dogs for the disabled approaches the century mark we must reconfirm the place of canine companions in the village square. There's nothing like having a serious, professionally trained dog when you've a disability. I don't even mind being called a "shill." I am an enthusiastic customer.

If you're a business owner the law does not force you to endure a misbehaving animal. In fact it's the performance of a service dog that really matters—not merely in traffic or in crowds, but everywhere. Not long ago a reporter for a New York tabloid took her own badly behaved dog into a famous restaurant, telling the manager she had a disability, knowing full well she didn't need to produce any proof. Then she ostentatiously encouraged her dog to eat off plates on tables. Her point? Anyone can bring his or her dog anywhere because of the specious ADA. Lost on this writer was the hoary fact that people can imitate anything in America. If you wish you can pretend to be a Rockefeller or dress as a priest. We've always been a nation of con men, and the able-bodied have often pretended to be disabled, imagining advantages like better parking or early boarding on airplanes. Here's what I suggest: look for the professionalism of the disabled and their companion animals and try to remember real working dogs are pros.

Throughout this memoir I've mentioned how Corky made me more self-accepting. Not everyone needs to have this kind of journey. In these times, post ADA, it's more likely one will train with a service dog simply as a helpmate, without the psychological elements I've described. To paraphrase Sigmund Freud, "sometimes a dog is just a dog."

I've had four dogs from Guiding Eyes for the Blind and I'm a proud alum of their program; however, there are a dozen guide-dog schools in the United States and they're equally good. You can read more about guide-dog training schools by visiting the website of the National Association of Guide Dog Users, which is a working group of the National Federation of the Blind. Their site can be found at: http://www.nagdu.org.

Acknowledgments

I wish to acknowledge the Blue Mountain Center, the MacDowell Colony, and the Saltonstall Foundation for residencies that greatly assisted me during the writing of this book.

Many friends, both blind and sighted, have helped me along the way. I owe special thanks to Melinda Angstrom, Bill Badger, Becky Barnes, Marvin Bell, Graham Buck, Eric Holzwarth, Arthur Krieck, Connie Kuusisto, James Lecesne, Michael Meteyer, William Peace, David Reilly, Jane Russenberger, Ralph Savarese, Diane Wiener, Ken Weisner, David Weiss, and Kathy Zubrycki. Crucial support was provided by my agent, Irene Skolnick, and by editors Karyn Marcus and Sydney Tanigawa.

About the Author

Stephen Kuusisto was born in Exeter, New Hampshire, in 1955. He is the author of the memoirs *Planet of the Blind* (a *New York Times* Notable Book of the Year), *Eavesdropping: A Life by Ear*, and of the poetry collections *Only Bread, Only Light* and *Letters to Borges*. He has also authored a book-length essay *Do Not Interrupt: A Playful Take on the Art of Conversation*. A graduate of the Iowa Writers' Workshop and a Fulbright Scholar, he has taught at the University of Iowa, Hobart and William Smith Colleges, and the Ohio State University. He currently teaches at Syracuse University. He lives in DeWitt, New York, with his wife, Connie. He is a frequent speaker in the United States and abroad. His website is: www.stephenkuusisto.com.

South Huntington

MAR 06 2018

DISCARD